Black Slave Narratives

BLACK SLAVE
NARRATIVES

EDITED AND WITH AN INTRODUCTION BY

John F. Bayliss

THE MACMILLAN COMPANY

COLLIER-MACMILLAN LTD., LONDON

The Macmillan Company
866 Third Avenue, New York, N.Y. 10022
Collier-Macmillan Canada Ltd., Toronto, Ontario

Library of Congress Catalog Card Number: 76-126190

First Printing

Printed in the United States of America

Contents

6 CONTENTS

The Women 108
1. HARRIET JACOBS 108
2. HARRIET TUBMAN 116
3. ELIZABETH KECKLEY 132

Superstition 147
1. HENRY BIBB 147
2. WILLIAM GRIMES 152

Adventure 156
1. JAMES THOMPSON 156
2. "UNCLE TOM'S BEAR FIGHT" 163

Revolt 166
1. NAT TURNER 166
2. HARRIET JACOBS 184

Escape 191
1. HENRY "BOX" BROWN 191
2. JAMES W. C. PENNINGTON 196

Introduction

Slavery is caught in the guts of America. No matter
how benevolent the Black may feel towards his white
American brother he can never obliterate from his
memory the fact that his ancestors were uprooted from
their country, albeit by their own people, and trans-
ported by whites to an alien land in chains. And as for
the white, as an individual and as a nation, he has to
probe his soul for depths of prejudice toward a colored
race. In *Democracy in America*, de Tocqueville wrote
of the dilemma:

The Negro transmits the eternal mark of his ignominy to
all his descendants; and although the law may abolish slavery, God alone can obliterate the traces of its existence.
The moderns then, after they have abolished slavery, have
three prejudices to contend against . . . the prejudice of
the master, the prejudice of the race and the prejudice of
color.

Some may contend that the malignant ulcer of slavery
formed a guilt complex in the white race for its inhumanity to man. This is a dubious contention and

8   BLACK SLAVE NARRATIVES

the result of slavery for the white is a smoldering distrust of his Black fellow American. The maturing of
the Black race in this country since Abolition has had
the force to send Uncle Tomism to the winds; even the
suffocating white liberalism has been tabooed. The
Black has matured the white attitude. One has only to
check Herman Melville's scornful jibes at the attitudes
of Delano, the northern captain, in "Benito Cereno"
to see how far we have come. Melville saw the North
basking in the innocence of its noble savage viewpoint.
For example, the captain saw the enslaved colored
women on the ghost ship as leopardesses curled up
with their cubs. Today, this attitude would be not only
anathema but unthinkable. No, what remains as the
residue of slavery is distrust and prejudice, so that
when provoked the white may say "Black" but think
"Nigger."

How does one escape this malignancy? De Tocqueville would leave the matter to God. Perhaps a combination of God above and honesty below would be a
more sincere solution. The Black must face his anger
to rise above it; the white must probe the slave past
to understand the Black present, to understand the extent of the accommodation to be made by both sides
to form a viable America. To shun the confrontation
makes both races less human, less great. To the extent that America is honest she is admired by other
nations; to the extent that the other nations are dis-
honest and shun their own racial problems, they are
loathsome to themselves.

One of the most meaningful confrontations with
slavery and its aftermath has been made in the music
of the Blues. As Ralph Ellison noted in *Shadow and
Act*, the Blues are:

. . . an impulse to keep the painful details and episodes of
a brutal experience alive in one's aching consciousness, to

finger its jagged grain, to transcend it, not by the consolation of philosophy but by squeezing from it a near-tragic, near-comic lyricism.

The slave narratives are the Blues in prose. They are the honest records of slave experience written by those who suffered under the system. The genre began with John Saffin's *Adam Negro's Tryall* in 1703 and has continued through the present as visitors to the recent exhibition, "Harlem on My Mind," held at the Metropolitan Museum of Art in New York City, saw on television screens the aged Mother Brown recording her impressions of life as a slave. The high water mark of this genre, however, came during the period 1830–1860. Benjamin Brawley, in *Early Negro Amerirican Writers* (1935), summed up succinctly this era of the slave narrative:

. . . about the year 1830 a profound change in the life of the Negro took place. Before that date the estate of the black man was so lowly that even personality was sometimes denied; after 1830, however, the Negro was an issue. On January 1, 1831, Garrison founded the *Liberator*, and in his addresses he appealed to the self-respect of the Negro. "Maintain your rights," he said, "in all cases, and at whatever expense. Wherever you are allowed to vote, see that your names are put on the list of voters, and go to the polls."

In 1833, the American Anti-Slavery Society was organized. The campaigning efforts of the Abolitionists were largely responsible for the rise of Frederick Douglass, William Wells Brown, and several other Negro orators of the next one or two decades. Brawley continued his observations by noting:

There was also inspiration from abroad. Hugo and Mazzini, Macauley and Mrs. Browning were now on the scene; and in 1833 slavery was abolished in the English dominions. It was a time of furious conflict, but also a time of infinite hope.

Egged on by this feeling of hope and by the commitment of the Abolitionists, the fugitive slave was under strong pressure to embellish his narrative, or let it be embellished for him. An article in the *Christian Examiner and Religious Miscellany* for September 1854 (which incidentally remains one of the best critical articles on the narratives and a key document in the controversy as to whether or not Father Henson was the inspiration for Uncle Tom in *Uncle Tom's Cabin*) discussed the nagging issue of authenticity. The Reverend Ephraim Peabody wrote:

America has the mournful honor of adding a new department to the literature of civilization,—the autobiographies of escaped slaves. We have placed below the titles of five narratives of this description. The subjects of two of these narratives, Douglass and Henson, we have known personally, and, apart from the internal evidence of truth which these stories afford, we have every reason to put confidence in them as men of veracity. The authors of the remaining accounts are, for anything we know to the contrary, equally trustworthy.

Many of the editions of the narratives had supporting evidence attached in the form of letters. The story of Harriet Tubman had many pages given over to correspondence; Frederick Douglass inserted the exchange of letters on the authenticity of his description of Covey, his harsh owner. As an example of copious documentation there is the introduction to the narrative of Henry Bibb. Besides a plethora of supporting letters, the writers of the introduction asserted:

To many, the elevated style, purity of diction, and easy flow of language, frequently exhibited, will appear unaccountable and contradictory, in view of his want of early mental culture. But to the thousands who have listened with delight to his speeches on anniversary and other occasions, these same traits will be noted as unequivocal evidence of originality. Very few men present in their written composition,

so perfect a transcript of their style as is exhibited by
Mr. Bibb.

Having hinted at two main issues in the study of the
slave narratives, namely their relevance and their authenticity, there remain two other key areas to be discussed: availability and approaches to study.

Ideally, an anthology should fire enough enthusiasm
to inspire the reader to go beyond its limitations into
the full body of the study. Unfortunately, the material
is difficult to come by. Where, in fact, is the access
road to a larger selection of the six thousand extant
narratives?

As to the availability of the material at the school
level, Julius Lester has compiled a careful anthology
of the Black Slave Narratives with gripping illustrations
by Tom Feelings. The book is entitled *To Be a Slave*
(The Dial Press, 1968) and should be of use to
the lower grades of high school. For even younger
students, the diligent librarian should turn up some pertinent titles. The World Publishing Company, for example, has recently published *Venture For Freedom*
(1969) by Ruby Zagoren, which is a simplified version
of the narrative of Venture Smith. There is also *Black
Bondage: The Life of Slaves in the South* (1969)
by Walter Goodman, published by Farrar, Straus and
Giroux.

For the mature reader, Arno Press and the Negro
Universities Press are both reprinting the narratives, the
latter extensively. But the volumes are expensive and
will be for the pockets of libraries. Fortunately,
publishers have begun to make the narratives available in paperback. The first four titles of a fugitive
slave series from Addison-Wesley Publishing Company
cover the narratives of Benjamin Drew, Josiah Henson,
Austin Steward, and William Wells Brown. Arno
Press has published a compendium of five narratives

under the editorship of William Loren Katz. Likewise, Beacon Press has published a compendium of three narratives under the editorship of Arna Bontemps. The narrative of Harriet Tubman is available from Corinth Books. For some time, the narrative of Frederick Douglass has been available in paperback; Macmillan, New American Library, Harvard University Press, Dover Publications, and Arno Press have editions. The prospective reader can become choosy about the introduction and original edition being used. Finally, Holt, Rinehart and Winston has produced *Life Under the Peculiar Institution* edited by N. Yetman which anthologizes narratives from the WPA Project material collected during the thirties.

Two unrivaled collections are those of the Schomburg Library (103 West 135th Street, New York City) and of the Moorland Library at Howard University, Washington, D.C. The definitive bibliography of the Black Slave Narratives, including the locations of library holdings and of secondary sources up to 1946, is to be found in an indispensable, but unpublished, doctoral dissertation from New York University (1946) by Marion Wilson Starling entitled "The Black Slave Narrative: Its Place in American Literary History." The bibliography covers pages 493 to 523. Microfilm copies only are available.

One of the more perplexing aspects in approaching the narratives is how to set about the actual study. The material is not only vast but capable of multiple treatment. It lends itself to historical interpretation, to social, psychological, folkloric, and literary considerations. The reader must decide on his focus.

For the placing of the narratives in a historical perspective, there is Charles H. Nichols' *Many Thousand Gone: The Ex-Slaves' Account of Their Bondage and Freedom* (Leiden, Netherlands, 1963 and Indiana University Press, 1969). The author quotes conservative estimates of the Negro slave intake for America: 900,000 in the sixteenth century, 2,750,000 in the seventeenth century, 7,000,000 in the eighteenth century, and 4,000,000 in the nineteenth century. He recalls how two of the "African" narrative writers, Venture Smith and Gustavus Vassa (Olaudah Equiano), had the misfortune to experience the Middle Passage under Captain Luke Collingwood. Vassa told Granville Sharp, an English Abolitionist, of conditions during an epidemic which the latter entered in his diary for March 9, 1783:

Gustavus Vassa called on me with an account of 132 Negroes being thrown into the sea from on board an English slave ship.

The matter was relayed to the Duke of Portland in such a manner that it became a *cause célèbre* "and probably rang the death knell of the English slave trade."

Nichols ably handles the vast amount of material afforded by the narratives by dividing his work into pertinent chapters. In the "Ole Massa" chapter, for example, he discusses the question of whether or not the slaves were happy under their masters and mistresses. He cites a list of eminent visitors to the South who left records of their findings: Fanny Kemble, Charles Lyell, Frederick Law Olmsted, Harriet Martineau, James Redpath, and Charles Dickens. The reader may care to juxtapose their accounts with the narratives (see Ball, p. 48). The author discusses the myth of Southern aristocracy in the light of the narratives and also in the light of subsequent white fiction. He notes the true pictures in the novels of Erskine Caldwell and G. W. Harris. "For their masters were the same coon-hunting, whiskey-drinking, tobacco-chewing crackers as the masses of poor whites. Though less indolent than he, they resemble Sut Lovingood." The anthology extracts highlight the debauchery and inhumanity of these owners and overseers (see Ball, p. 48; John Brown, Henson, Northup and Roper). There are other entries, however, which show slaves living in reasonable contentment with their masters (see Aunt Clara Davis; also Ball, who shows an ambivalent attitude toward his owners, p. 48). As a limited task, the evidence of the narratives could be put alongside such a pro-Southern work as John Herbert Nelson's *Negro Character in American Literature* (1926). Discussing Frederick Douglass, for example, Nelson asserts:

Douglass's well written narrative, grossly unfair to Southern life and people, is yet highly meaningful in showing how an intelligent man—a man whose mental contribution was Anglo-Saxon, whose will was with the white man's also—how such a man reacted to being classed as another man's property.

But, while upholding the South with his cryptic insertion, Nelson unconsciously flays the South with the rest of his statement.

The historian, interested in the economic aspects of slavery, should find ample evidence in the narratives to elucidate the causes of economic blight brought on by the shortsightedness of the Southern slave owners (see Ball, p. 48).

Miscegenation is yet another abuse which Nichols treats in his chapter entitled "Ole Massa." Starling noted of the mulatto:

Far from enjoying a favored position in the slaveholder's household, in recognition of his mixed blood, the lot of the mulatto slave was usually harder than that of the other slaves on the plantation, if he was a male . . . but the usual outlook for the mulatto slave woman, especially if she possessed striking beauty, which many of them did, was sale, sometimes at prices ranging from twelve hundred to as high as *eight thousand* dollars, for licentious purposes that were the heartbreak of the helpless girl and her saddened parents.

This anthology shows Moses Roper, a mulatto narrative writer, faring very badly despite his part white origins. As for the schemes of the master, there is the evidence of Harriet Jacobs's narrative—which reads like Samuel Richardson's eighteen-century novel, *Pamela*.

The "African" narratives, those accounts which deal in part with life in Africa before transportation to America, may well be of interest to readers with a historical bias. Only about four of these narratives are extant. Another narrative, that of Zamba, although a lively account of a young African prince, is considered essentially fictional. Philip D. Curtin's *Africa Remembered: Narratives by West Africans from the Era of the Slave Trade* (1967), is a useful tool here because it elaborates on the material by including narratives by slaves with other destinations than America. The chapter on Olaudah Equiano (Gustavus Vassa) is of great interest since G. I. Jones tracks down the actual locations of this slave's African history. By adding Augusta Juanita Johnson's thesis, "An Introduction to the Autobiography of Gustavus Vassa" (see the Schomburg Library), the reader should be well on the way to garnering a full background. For those who wish to move into a larger preoccupation with African narratives, Curtin has provided an interesting bibliography.

The comparative study of Africa and America, Afro-American Studies in fact, raises some challenging, fundamental issues with regard to the viability of these studies. The reader may well find himself burrowing into a recent pioneering work such as *Neo-African Literature: A History of Black Writing* (1968) by Janheinz Jahn, to see if any scholarly connections can be made in a study of the literatures of the two countries.

Another line of inquiry concerning the African narratives is more psychological than historical. Vernon Loggins, in *The Negro Author* (1931) refers to the African narrator as being more carefree, more adventuresome than his Anglo-Saxon counterpart. For example, he analyzes the outlook of Vassa by stating:

Vassa remained the African, gifted with an imagination which foreign environment could not destroy. His temperament was not made over again by the civilization with which he came in contact, and which he seems always to have evaluated according to his native African standards. One feels in his pages the Negro's mysticism, his unquestioning acceptance of the strange, his genius for adapting himself, his almost uncanny common-sense insight into the characters of those around him, his spirit of laughing resignation when in adversity, and his fully awake sensitiveness to the concreteness of life.

A Frederick Douglass or a William Wells Brown was a man of a very different mold.

Continuing the suggestions for psychological approaches to the study of the narratives, an unpublished doctoral dissertation from Indiana University (1967) by Gladys M. Fry, entitled "The Night Riders: A Study in the Social Control of the Negro," provides a model of research around a psychological cluster; in this case, the system for frightening the slaves. Miss Fry sums up her thesis in the following words:

The folk history of the Negro based on oral tradition throws light on the use of psychological control based on a fear of the supernatural. This system has one primary aim—to discourage the unauthorized movement of Negroes, especially at night. It was accompanied by indoctrinating Negroes with a fear of encountering supernatural things.

During slavery the system was used to prevent insurrections by discouraging the assembly of Negroes. In the post-Civil War period to the time of World War I this method was employed to stem the tide of the Negro movement from rural farming areas in the South to the cities of the North. The form of this technique of supernatural control and the manner in which it was employed by the Southern whites constitute one aspect of an unrecorded Negro folk history of that period.

This anthology provides stark evidence for the control of slaves by fear (see Bibb, p. 147).

On the other hand, in a narrative like "Uncle Tom's Bear Fight," the fear of the supernatural is transmuted into a craftiness that is of the very essence of Negro folklore in America. An important work for the discussion of the folklore aspect of the narratives is B. A. Botkin's *Lay My Burden Down: A Folk History of Slavery* (1945). The author, who was the director of the WPA project which in the thirties collected a mountain of orally recorded slave narratives, ably summarizes the contribution of the narratives to the folklorist.

In its static structure, "extra-organizational" and "extra-technological," slave society was a folk society, here revealed in all its multiplicity of folkways and folk notions, differentiated by occupation, region, and economy—field hand, house servant, and artisan; Sea Islands, Tidewater, and Deep South; cotton, tobacco, and sugar plantations. As a self-taught, self-contained group, moreover, on the make-it-yourself-or-do-without level of culture, slaves had their folk handskills and mindskills, their play of popular fantasy in both the real and the unreal world, their songs, stories, sayings, games, pastimes, and superstitious beliefs and practices. Finally, slaves had their own code of behavior with respect to the whites, to complement the latter's slave code; and ex-slaves have kept alive their own tradition of slavery to match the white plantation tradition. As a mixture of fact and fiction, then, colored by the fantasy and idealization of old people recalling the past, the narratives constitute a kind of collective saga of slavery.

Finally, there is the literary study of the Black Slave Narratives. B. A. Botkin has some very enlightening observations on how the narratives were collected for his project and how the dialects were preserved. His comments would seem essential to a discussion of the style of the narratives. (The WPA project material may be inspected at the Library of Congress. The Schomburg Library has microfilm copies of the narratives.)

Both Nichols and Starling devote some space to the origins of *Uncle Tom's Cabin*; both refer to fiction stemming from the slave narratives, and both argue that characterization should be a key consideration in a study of the literary merits, and demerits, of the narratives. Nichols has two purple pages in which he calls the roster of the slave narrators, juxtaposing them to show the diversity of their characters and of their experiences. Although the title of Starling's thesis implies a search for the literary place of the narratives, the work shows little evidence of this particular inquiry. The author is hardly sanguine in the introduction to the only chapter specifically on the topic.

The slave narratives, on the whole, are admittedly low in aesthetic values. They possess primary significance for the social historian, in their picture of the institution of slavery as seen through the eyes of the bondsman himself. Some of the narratives achieve a degree of literary distinction, in passages; and the narratives of Equiano and Douglass are readily accessible as literary achievements.

Starling is being unfair here since the narratives do show a diversity of interesting styles. The phenomenal sales of the narratives were not entirely the result of Abolitionist fever. The leading narratives, such as those of Douglass, William Wells Brown, Ball, Bibb, Henson, Northup, Pennington, and Roper deserve to be considered for a place in American literature, a place beyond the merely historical. The reader will come to his own conclusions.

A paradox may exist here. The narrative of Frederick Douglass enjoyed the largest sales in the last century and is the most readily accessible today. But as literature, the narrative may be of lesser importance. Douglass was a great rhetorician—he was actually an operator of bellows in a brass foundry when the pioneer Abolitionist, William Lloyd Garrison, came upon him in New Bedford—and his prose is likewise rhetorical. As a narrative, his style is flawed. It is even possible he had a deleterious effect on subsequent Black writing until the Harlem Renaissance. Though never slaves, both W. E. B. DuBois and James Weldon Johnson possessed an ability to interrupt their novels in order to launch a Douglass tirade at the reader. The paradox is that the author with the greatest verbal talent did not seem to have a corresponding ability in prose; or rather, that his ability at oration smothered his ability to write.

The Starling thesis, while skirting critical approaches to the literary quality of the narratives, is of particular use in its discussion of slave narrative-writing as a genre, co-existing with the other literary movements of the times. In the eighteenth century, the thesis points out, the genre eddied about in company with narratives of a picaresque type. At the end of the century, these slave accounts gained their first significance in Britain, and then in America, as vehicles of propaganda. By the late 1840s, a critic was able to record that they formed "a new department to the literature of civilization." In the early 1850s, a fellow critic dubbed them, "those literary nigritudes—little tadpoles of the press . . . which run to editions of hundreds of thousands."

Of particular interest is Starling's treatment of the revolution in printing which enabled the slave narratives to flood the market.

It was not by way of inspiration from reasoned addresses and indefatigable efforts for the adoption of gradual emancipation plans that slavery was destined to be scotched; but by way of one of the most recent of the industrial inventions revolutionizing the harnessing of steam to the printing press, which led immediately to the production of journals for the masses.

Whereas, up to the middle of the 1820s only the rich could afford newspapers at a five to eight dollar subscription annually, by 1828 the "penny newspaper" was on the market. As Arthur Schlesinger noted, "It was the most abundant outpouring the nation had ever known and a documentary revelation of the many-sided American mind such as existed in no earlier period."

This introduction opened with a discussion of the relevance of the narratives. If current affairs are the ultimate in relevance, then those with literary bias may care to follow the raging controversy surrounding William Styron's bestseller, *The Confessions of Nat Turner* (1966). Here is a white novelist daring to write a story based on the recorded narrative of a mystic insurrectionist slave. Black critics were loud in their condemnation, and their collected views are to be found in *William Styron's Nat Turner: 10 Black Writers Respond* (1968). The debate has raised some valuable basic considerations about how far the novelist may tamper with history in the interests of his art.

For those readers drawn to comparative literature studies, a fruitful avenue of inquiry may be found in comparing American Slave Narratives with Australian Convict Narratives. By coincidence, a recent bestseller in Australia, *Bring Larks and Heroes* (Viking Press, 1967), by Tom Keneally, is a story about convicts whose lot much resembled that of the Black American slaves.

As for approaches to study, the possibilities seem endless; and enthralling.

Bloomington, 1970

JOHN F. BAYLISS

Black Slave Narratives

The Africans

•••-•••-•••-•••-•••-•••-•••-•••-•••-•••-•••-•••-•••-•••-•••-•••-•

Born in 1745, GUSTAVUS VASSA wrote his popular narrative
for publication in 1788. In his thesis, Starling lists U.S.
library holdings for fourteen of the thirty-six editions which
had appeared by the mid-1850s. Cited is the 1790 third
London edition of *The Interesting Narrative of the Life of
Olaudah Equiano, or Gustavus Vassa, the African; by Himself*. VENTURE SMITH, an uncommonly capable person, also
narrated his African past. The narrative was first published
in 1798. A reprinted 1835 edition, which bears some of the
primitivistic clichés of the time, is cited. CHARLES BALL was
the first fugitive slave to have a full-length work published
under the sponsorship of the Abolitionists. After initially
heavy sales, the work was spurned for twenty years owing
to an authenticity dispute. The extract, taken from an 1860
Dayton edition, shows how the African culture continued
on in America.

1

I was born in the city of Bournou; my mother was the
eldest daughter of the reigning King of Zaara, of which

Bournou is the chief city. I was the youngest of six children, and particularly loved by my mother, and my grandfather almost doted on me.

I had, from my infancy, a curious turn of mind, was more grave and reserved in my disposition than either of my brothers and sisters. I often teased them with questions they could not answer; for which reason they disliked me, as they supposed that I was either foolish, or insane. 'Twas certain that I was, at times, very unhappy in myself: it being strongly impressed on my mind, that there was some GREAT MAN of power, which resided above the sun, moon, and stars, the objects of our worship. My dear indulgent mother would bear more with me than any of my friends beside. I often raised my hands to heaven, and asked her who lived there? was much dissatisfied when she told me the sun, moon, and stars, being persuaded, in my own mind, that there must be some Superior Power.—I was frequently lost in wonder at the works of the creation: was afraid, uneasy, and restless, but could not tell for what. I wanted to be informed of things that no person could tell me; and was always dissatisfied. These wonderful impressions began in my childhood, and followed me continually till I left my parents, which affords me matter of admiration and thankfulness.

To this moment I grew more and more uneasy every day, insomuch, that one Saturday, (which is the day on which we keep our Sabbath) I labored under anxieties and fears that cannot be expressed; and, what is more extraordinary, I could not give a reason for it. I rose, as our custom is, about three o'clock, (as we are obliged to be at our place of worship an hour before sunrise:) We say nothing in our worship, but continue on our knees with our hands held up, observing a strict silence till the sun is at a certain height, which I suppose to be about ten or eleven o'clock in England:

when, at a certain sign made by the priest, we get up (our duty being over,) and disperse to our different houses. Our place of meeting is under a large palm tree; we divide ourselves into many congregations; as it is impossible for the same tree to cover the inhabitants of the whole city, though they are extremely large, high and majestic; the beauty and usefulness of them are not to be described; they supply the inhabitants of the country with meat, drink, and clothes;* the body of the palm tree is very large; at a certain season of the year they tap it, and bring vessels to receive the wine, of which they draw great quantities, the quality of which is very delicious; the leaves of this tree are of a silky nature; they are large and soft: when they are dried and pulled to pieces, it has much the same appearance as the English flax, and the inhabitants of Bournou manufacture it for clothing, etc. This tree likewise produces a plant, or substance, which has the appearance of a cabbage, and very like it, in taste almost the same: it grows between the branches. Also the palm tree produces a nut, something like a cocoa nut, which contains a kernel, in which is a large quantity of milk, very pleasant to the taste: the shell is of a hard substance, and of a very beautiful appearance, and serves for basons, bowls, etc.

I hope this digression will be forgiven. I was going to observe, that after the duty of our Sabbath was over (on the day in which I was more distressed and afflicted than ever) we were all on our way home as usual, when a remarkable black cloud arose and covered the sun; then followed very heavy rain, and thunder more dreadful than ever I had heard: the heavens roared, and the earth trembled at it: I was

* It is a general received opinion, in England, that the natives of Africa go entirely unclothed, but this supposition is very unjust: they have a kind of dress so as to appear decent, though it is very slight and thin.

highly affected and cast down: insomuch that I wept
sadly; and could not follow my relations and friends
home. I was obliged to stop, and felt as if my legs
were tied, they seemed to shake under me: so I stood
still, being in great fear of the Man of Power, that I
was persuaded in myself lived above. One of my young
companions (who entertained a particular friendship
for me, and I for him) came back to see for me: he
asked me why I stood still in such very hard rain? I
only said to him that my legs were weak, and I could
not come faster: he was much affected to see me cry,
and took me by the hand, and said he would lead me
home, which he did. My mother was greatly alarmed
at my tarrying out in such terrible weather; she asked
me many questions, such as what I did so for, and if
I was well? My dear mother, says I, pray tell me who
is the great Man of Power that makes the thunder?
She said, there was no power but the sun, moon, and
stars; that they made all our country. I then inquired
how all our people came? She answered me, from one
another; and so carried me to many generations back.
Then says I, who made the *first man?* and who made
the first cow, and the first lion, and where does the fly
come from, as no man can make him? My mother
seemed in great trouble; she was apprehensive that my
senses were impaired, or that I was foolish. My father
came in, and seeing her in grief asked the cause, but
when she related our conversation to him, he was exceedingly angry with me, and told me he would punish
me severely, if ever I was so troublesome again; so
that I resolved never to say any thing more to him.
But I grew very unhappy in myself; my relations and
acquaintance endeavoured, by all the means they
could think on, to divert me, by taking me to ride on
goats, (which is much the custom of our country) and
to shoot with a bow and arrow; but I experienced no
satisfaction at all in any of these things; nor could I be

easy by any means whatever; my parents were very
unhappy to see me so dejected and melancholy.

About this time there came a merchant from the
Gold Coast (the third city in Guinea) he traded with
the inhabitants of our country in ivory, etc., he took
great notice of my unhappy situation, and inquired into
the cause; he expressed vast concern for me, and said,
if my parents would part with me for a little while,
and let him take me home with him, it would be of
more service to me than any thing they could do for
me. He told me that if I would go with him, I should
see houses with wings to them walk upon the water,
and should also see the white folks; and that he had
many sons nearly of my age, which should be my
companions; and he added to all this, that he would
bring me safe back again soon. I was highly pleased
with the account of this strange place, and was very
desirous of going. I seemed sensible of a secret impulse upon my mind, which I could not resist, that
seemed to tell me I must go. When my dear mother
saw I was willing to leave them, she spoke to my
father and grandfather, and the rest of my relations,
who all agreed that I should accompany the merchant
to the Gold Coast. I was the more willing as my
brothers and sisters despised me, and looked on me
with contempt, on the account of my unhappy disposition; and even my servants slighted me, and disregarded all I said to them. I had one sister who was
always exceeding fond of me, and I loved her entirely;
her name was Logwy, she was quite white, and fair,
with fine light hair, though my father and mother were
black. I was truly concerned to leave my beloved sister,
and she cried most sadly to part with me, wringing
her hands, and discovered every sign of grief that can
be imagined, indeed if I could have known when I left
my friends and country, that I should never return to
them again, my misery on that occasion would have

been inexpressible. All my relations were sorry to part with me; my dear mother came with me on a camel more than three hundred miles, the first of our journey lay chiefly through woods: at nights we secured ourselves from the wild beasts by making fires all around us; we and our camels kept within the circle, or we must have been torn to pieces by the lions, and other wild creatures, that roared terribly as soon as night came on, and continued to do so till morning. There can be little said in favor of the country through which we passed; only a valley of marble that we came through, which is unspeakably beautiful. On each side of this valley are exceeding high and almost inaccessible mountains. Some of these pieces of marble are of a prodigious length and breadth, but of different sizes and color, and shaped in a variety of forms, in a wonderful manner. It is most of it veined with gold, mixed with striking and beautiful colors; so that when the sun darts upon it, it is as pleasing a sight as can be imagined. The merchant that brought me from Bournou, was in partnership with another gentleman who accompanied us; he was very unwilling that he should take me from home, as, he said, he foresaw many difficulties that would attend my going with them. He endeavoured to prevail on the merchant to throw me into a very deep pit that was in the valley, but he refused to listen to him, and said, he was resolved to take care of me; but the other was greatly dissatisfied; and when we came to a river, which we were obliged to pass through, he purposed throwing me in and drowning me; but the merchant would not consent to it, so that I was preserved.

We travelled till about four o'clock every day, and then began to make preparations for night, by cutting down large quantities of wood, to make fires to preserve us from the wild beasts. I had a very unhappy and discontented journey, being in continual fear that

the people I was with would murder me. I often reflected with extreme regret on the kind friends I had
left, and the idea of my dear mother frequently drew
tears from my eyes. I cannot recollect how long we
were going from Bournou to the Gold Coast; but as
there is no shipping nearer Bournou than that city, it
was tedious in travelling so far by land, being upwards
of a thousand miles. I was heartily rejoiced when we
arrived at the end of our journey: I now vainly imagined that all my troubles and inquietudes would terminate here; but could I have looked into futurity, I
should have perceived that I had much more to suffer
than I had before experienced, and that they had as yet
barely commenced.

I was now more than a thousand miles from home,
without a friend, or means to procure one. Soon after
I came to the merchant's house, I heard the drums
beat remarkably loud, and the trumpets blow, the persons accustomed to this employ, are obliged to go on a
very high structure, appointed for that purpose, that the
sound may be heard at a great distance; they are
higher than the steeples in England. I was mightily
pleased with sounds so entirely new to me, and was
very inquisitive to know the cause of this rejoicing, and
asked many questions concerning it; I was answered
that it was meant as a compliment to me, because I
was Grandson to the King of Bournou.

This account gave me a secret pleasure; but I was
not suffered long to enjoy this satisfaction, for in the
evening of the same day, two of the merchant's sons
(boys about my own age) came running to me, and
told me, that the next day I was to die, for the king
intended to behead me. I replied, that I was sure it
could not be true, for I came there to play with them;
and to see houses walk upon the water with wings to
them, and the white folks; but I was soon informed
that their king imagined I was sent by my father as a

spy, and would make such discoveries at my return home, as would enable them to make war with greater advantage to ourselves; and for these reasons he had resolved I should never return to my native country. When I heard this, I suffered misery that cannot be described. I wished a thousand times that I had never left my friends and country. But still the Almighty was pleased to work miracles for me.

The morning I was to die, I was washed, and all my gold ornaments made bright and shining, and then carried to the palace, where the king was to behead me himself (as is the custom of the place). He was seated upon a throne at the top of an exceeding large yard, or court, which you must go through to enter the palace; it is as wide and spacious as a large field in England. I had a lane of lifeguards to go through; I guessed it to be about three hundred paces.

I was conducted by my friend the merchant, about half way up; then he durst proceed no farther: I went up to the king alone. I went with an undaunted courage, and it pleased God to melt the heart of the King, who sat with his cimeter in his hand ready to behead me; yet, being himself so affected, he dropped it out of his hand, and took me upon his knees, and wept over me. I put my right hand round his neck, and pressed him to my heart. He set me down and blessed me; and added, that he would not kill me, that I should not go home, but be sold for a slave, so then I was conducted back again to the merchant's house.

The next day he took me on board a French brig; but the captain did not choose to buy me; he said I was too small; so the merchant took me home with him again.

The partner, whom I have spoken of as my enemy, was very angry to see me return, and again proposed putting an end to my life; for he represented to the other, that I should bring them into troubles and dif-

ficulties, and that I was so little that no person would
buy me.

The merchant's resolution began to waver, and I was
indeed afraid that I should be put to death: but however, he said he would try me once more.

A few days after a Dutch ship came into the harbour, and they carried me on board, in hopes that the
captain would purchase me. As they went, I heard
them agree, that if they could not sell me *then*, they
would throw me overboard. I was in extreme agony
when I heard this; and as soon as ever I saw the
Dutch captain, I ran to him, and put my arms round
him, and said, "Father, save me;" (for I knew that if
he did not buy me, I should be treated very ill, or possibly murdered.) And though he did not understand
my language, yet it pleased the Almighty to influence
him in my behalf, and he bought me *for two yards of
check*, which is of more value *there*, than in England.

When I left my dear mother, I had a large quantity
of gold about me, as is the custom of our country, it
was made into rings, and they were linked into one
another, and formed into a kind of chain, and so put
round my neck, and arms and legs, and a large piece
hanging at one ear, almost in the shape of a pear. I
found all this troublesome, and was glad when my new
master took it from me. I was now washed and
clothed in the Dutch or English manner. My master
grew very fond of me, and I loved him exceedingly;
I watched every look, was always ready when he
wanted me, and endeavoured to convince him, by
every action, that my only pleasure was to serve him
well. I have since thought that he must have been a
serious man. His actions corresponded very well with
such a character. He used to read prayers in public to
the ship's crew every Sabbath day; and when first I saw
him read, I was never so surprised in my life, as when
I saw the book talk to my master, for I thought it

did, as I observed him to look upon it, and move his lips. I wished it would do so to me. As soon as my master had done reading, I followed him to the place where he put the book, being mightily delighted with it, and when nobody saw me, I opened it, and put my ear down close upon it, in great hopes that it would say something to me; but was very sorry, and greatly disappointed when I found it would not speak, this thought immediately presented itself to me, that every body and every thing despised me because I was black.

I was exceedingly sea-sick at first; but when I became more accustomed to the sea, it wore off. My master's ship was bound for Barbadoes. When we came there, he thought fit to speak of me to several gentlemen of his acquaintance, and one of them expressed a particular desire to see me. He had a great mind to buy me; but the Captain could not immediately be prevailed on to part with me; but however, as the gentleman seemed very solicitous, he at length let me go, and I was sold for fifty dollars (*four and sixpenny pieces in English*). My new master's name was Vanhorn, a young gentleman; his home was in New-England, in the city of New-York, to which place he took me with him. He dressed me in his livery, and was very good to me. My chief business was to wait at table and tea, and clean knives, and I had a very easy place; but the servants used to curse and swear surprisingly; which I learned faster than any thing, it was almost the first English I could speak. If any of them affronted me, I was sure to call upon God, to damn them immediately; but I was broke off it all at once, occasioned by the correction of an old black servant that lived in the family. One day I had just cleaned the knives for dinner, when one of the maids took one to cut bread and butter with; I was very angry with her, and immediately called upon God to damn her; when this old black man told me I must not say so. I asked him why? He replied that there was a wicked man called the Devil, who lived in hell, and would take all who said these words, and put them into the fire and burn them. This terrified me greatly, and I was entirely broke off swearing. Soon after this, as I was placing the china for tea, my mistress came into the room just as the maid had been cleaning it; the girl had unfortunately sprinkled the wainscot with the mop, at which my mistress was very angry, the girl very foolishly answered her again, which made her worse, and she called upon God to damn her. I was vastly concerned to hear this, as she was a fine young lady, and very good to me, insomuch that I could not help speaking to her; "Madam, says I, you must not say so." Why, said she? Because there is a black man called the Devil that lives in hell, and he will put you into the fire and burn you, and I shall be very sorry for that. Who told you this, replied my lady? Old Ned, says I. Very well, was all her answer; but she told my master of it, and he ordered that old Ned should be tied up and whipped, and he was never suffered to come into the kitchen with the rest of the servants afterwards. My mistress was not angry with me, but rather diverted with my simplicity, and by way of talk, she repeated what I had said to many of her acquaintance that visited her; among the rest Mr. Freelandhouse, a very gracious, good Minister, heard it, and he took a great deal of notice of me, and desired my master to part with me to him. He would not hear of it at first, but being greatly persuaded, he let me go, and Mr. Freelandhouse gave fifty pounds for me.—He took me home with him, and made me kneel down, and put my two hands together, and prayed for me, and every night and morning he did the same.—I could not make out what he did this for, nor the meaning of it, nor what they spoke to when they talked.—I thought it comical, but I liked it very well. After I had been a little while with my new master, I grew more familiar, and asked him the meaning of prayer, (I could hardly speak English to be understood) he took great pains with me, and made me understand that he prayed to God, who lived in heaven; that he was my Father and best Friend. I told him that this must be a mistake; that *my* father lived at Bournou, and that I wanted very much to see him, and likewise my dear mother, and sister, and I wished he would be so good as to send me home to them; and I added all that I could think of to induce him to convey me back. I appeared in great trouble, and my good master was so affected, that the tears ran down his face. He told me that God was a Great and Good Spirit, that He created all the world, and every person and thing in it, in Ethiopia, Africa, and America, and every where. I was delighted when I heard this: There, says I, I always thought so when I lived at home! Now if I had wings like an eagle, I would fly to tell my dear mother that God is greater than the sun, moon, and stars; and that they were made by Him.

GUSTAVUS VASSA

2

I was born at Dukandarra, in Guinea, about the year 1729. My father's name was Saungm Furro, Prince of the tribe of Dukandara. My father had three wives. Polygamy was not uncommon in that country, especially among the rich, as every man was allowed to keep as many wives as he could maintain. By his first wife he had three children. The eldest of them was myself, named by my father, Broteer. The other two were named Cundazo and Soozaduka. My father had two children by his second wife, and one by his third. I descended from a very large, tall and stout race of beings, much larger than the generality of people in other parts of the globe, being commonly considerable above six feet in height, and every way well proportioned.

The first thing worthy of notice which I remember was, a contention between my father and mother, on account of my father marrying his third wife without the consent of his first and eldest, which was contrary to the custom generally observed among my countrymen. In consequence of this rupture, my mother left her husband and country, and travelled away with her three children to the eastward. I was then five years old. She took not the least sustenance along with her, to support either herself or children. I was able to travel along by her side; the other two of her offspring she carried one on her back, and the other being a sucking child, in her arms. When we became hungry, our mother used to set us down on the ground, and gather some of the fruits which grew spontaneously in that climate. These served us for food on the way. At night we all lay down together in the most secure place we could find, and reposed ourselves until morning. Though there were many noxious animals there; yet so kind was our Almighty protector, that none of them were ever permitted to hurt or molest us. Thus we went on our journey until the second day after our departure from Dukandarra, when we came to the entrance of a great desert. During our travel in that we were often affrighted with the doleful howlings and yellings of wolves, lions, and other animals. After five days travel we came to the end of this desert, and immediately entered into a beautiful and extensive interval country. Here my mother was pleased to stop and seek a refuge for me. She left me at the house of a very rich farmer. I was then, as I should judge, not less than one hundred and forty miles from my native place, separated from all my relations and acquaintance. At this place my mother took her farewell of me, and set out for my own country. My new guardian, as I shall call the man with whom I was left, put me into the business of tending sheep, immediately after I was left with him. The flock which I kept with the assistance of a boy, consisted of about forty. We drove them every morning between two and three miles to pasture, into the wide and delightful plains. When night drew on, we drove them home and secured them in the cote. In this round I continued during my stay here. One incident which befell me when I was driving my flock from pasture, was so dreadful to me in that age, and is to this time so fresh in my memory, that I cannot help noticing it in this place. Two large dogs sallied out of a certain house and set upon me. One of them took me by the arm, and the other by the thigh, and before their master could come and relieve me, they lacerated my flesh to such a degree, that the scars are very visible to the present day. My master was immediately sent for. He came and carried me home, as I was unable to go myself on account of my wounds. Nothing remarkable happened afterwards until my father sent for me to return home.

Before I dismiss this country, I must just inform my reader what I remember concerning this place. A large river runs through this country in a westerly course. The land for a great way on each side is flat and level, hedged in by a considerable rise in the country at a great distance from it. It scarce ever rains there, yet the land is fertile; great dews fall in the night which refresh the soil. About the latter end of June or first of July, the river begins to rise, and gradually increases until it has inundated the country for a great distance, to the height of seven or eight feet. This brings on a slime which enriches the land surprisingly. When the river has subsided, the natives begin to sow and plant, and the vegetation is exceeding rapid. Near this rich river my guardian's land lay. He possessed, I cannot exactly tell how much, yet this I am certain of respecting it, that he owned an immense tract. He possessed likewise a great many cattle and goats. During my stay with him I was kindly used, and with as much tenderness, for what I saw, as his only son, although I was an entire stranger to him, remote from friends and relations. The principal occupations of the inhabitants there, were the cultivation of the soil and the care of their flocks. They were a people pretty similar in every respect to that of mine, except in their persons, which were not so tall and stout. They appeared to be very kind and friendly. I will now return to my departure from that place.

My father sent a man and horse after me. After settling with my guardian for keeping me, he took me away and went for home. It was then about one year since my mother brought me here. Nothing remarkable occurred to us on our journey until we arrived safe home.

I found then that the difference between my parents had been made up previous to their sending for me. On my return, I was received both by my father and mother with great joy and affection, and was once more restored to my paternal dwelling in peace and happiness. I was then about six years old.

Not more than six weeks had passed after my return, before a message was brought by an inhabitant of the place where I lived the preceding year to my father, that that place had been invaded by a numerous army, from a nation not far distant, furnished with musical instruments, and all kinds of arms then in use; that they were instigated by some white nation who equipped and sent them to subdue and possess the country; that his nation had made no preparation for war, having been for a long time in profound peace; that they could not defend themselves against such a

formidable train of invaders, and must therefore neces-
sarily evacuate their lands to the fierce enemy, and fly
to the protection of some chief; and that if he would
permit them they would come under his rule and protection when they had to retreat from their own
possessions. He was a kind and merciful prince, and
therefore consented to these proposals.

He had scarcely returned to his nation with the message, before the whole of his people were obliged to
retreat from their country, and come to my father's
dominions.

He gave them every privilege and all the protection
his government could afford. But they had not been
there longer than four days before news came to them
that the invaders had laid waste their country, and
were coming speedily to destroy them in my father's
territories. This affrighted them, and therefore they
immediately pushed off to the southward, into the unknown countries there, and were never more heard of.

Two days after their retreat, the report turned out
to be but too true. A detachment from the enemy came
to my father and informed him, that the whole army
was encamped not far out of his dominions, and would
invade the territory and deprive his people of their lib-
erties and rights, if he did not comply with the following terms. These were to pay them a large sum of
money, three hundred fat cattle, and a great number
of goats, sheep, asses, etc.

My father told the messenger he would comply
rather than that his subjects should be deprived of their
rights and privileges, which he was not then in circumstances to defend from so sudden an invasion.
Upon turning out those articles, the enemy pledged
their faith and honor that they would not attack him.
On these he relied and therefore thought it unneces-
sary to be on his guard against the enemy. But their
pledges of faith and honor proved no better than those

of other unprincipled hostile nations; for a few days after a certain relation of the king came and informed him, that the enemy who sent terms of accommodation to him and received tribute to their satisfaction, yet meditated an attack upon his subjects by surprise and that probably they would commence their attack in less than one day, and concluded with advising him, as he was not prepared for war, to order a speedy retreat of his family and subjects. He complied with this advice.

The same night which was fixed upon to retreat, my father and his family set off about the break of day. The king and his two younger wives went in one company, and my mother and her children in another. We left our dwellings in succession, and my father's company went on first. We directed our course for a large shrub plain, some distance off, where we intended to conceal ourselves from the approaching enemy, until we could refresh ourselves a little. But we presently found that our retreat was not secure. For having struck up a little fire for the purpose of cooking victuals, the enemy who happened to be encamped a little distance off, had sent out a scouting party who discovered us by the smoke of the fire, just as we were extinguishing it, and about to eat. As soon as we had finished eating, my father discovered the party, and immediately began to discharge arrows at them. This was what I first saw, and it alarmed both me and the women, who being unable to make any resistance, immediately betook ourselves to the tall thick reeds not far off, and left the old king to fight alone. For some time I beheld him from the reeds defending himself with great courage and firmness, till at last he was obliged to surrender himself into their hands.

They then came to us in the reeds, and the very first salute I had from them was a violent blow on the back part of the head with the fore part of a gun, and at the same time a grasp round the neck. I then had a rope put about my neck, as had all the women in the thicket with me, and were immediately led to my father, who was likewise pinioned and haltered for leading. In this condition we were all led to the camp. The women and myself being pretty submissive, had tolerable treatment from the enemy, while my father was closely interrogated respecting his money which they knew he must have. But as he gave them no account of it, he was instantly cut and pounded on his body with great inhumanity, that he might be induced by the torture he suffered to make the discovery. All this availed not in the least to make him give up his money, but he despised all the tortures which they inflicted, until the continued exercise and increase of torment, obliged him to sink and expire. He thus died without informing his enemies where his money lay. I saw him while he was thus tortured to death. The shocking scene is to this day fresh in my mind, and I have often been overcome while thinking on it. He was a man of remarkable stature. I should judge as much as six feet and six or seven inches high, two feet across his shoulders, and every way well proportioned. He was a man of remarkable strength and resolution, affable, kind and gentle, ruling with equity and moderation.

The army of the enemy was large, I should suppose consisting of about six thousand men. Their leader was called Baukurre. After destroying the old prince, they decamped and immediately marched towards the sea, lying to the west, taking with them myself and the women prisoners. In the march a scouting party was detached from the main army. To the leader of this party I was made waiter, having to carry his gun, etc. As we were a scouting we came across a herd of fat cattle, consisting of about thirty in number. These we set upon, and immediately wrested from their keepers, and afterwards converted them into food for the army. The enemy had remarkable success in destroying the country wherever they went. For as far as they had penetrated, they laid the habitations waste and captured the people. The distance they had now brought me was about four hundred miles. All the march I had very hard tasks imposed on me, which I must perform on pain of punishment. I was obliged to carry on my head a large flat stone used for grinding our corn, weighing as I should suppose, as much as twenty-five pounds; besides victuals, mat and cooking utensils. Though I was pretty large and stout at my age, yet these burdens were very grievous to me, being only six years and a half old.

We were then come to a place called Malagasco. When we entered the place we could not see the least appearance of either houses or inhabitants, but upon stricter search found, that instead of houses above ground they had dens in the sides of hillocks, contiguous to ponds and streams of water. In these we perceived they had all hid themselves, as I suppose they usually did on such occasions. In order to compel them to surrender, the enemy contrived to smoke them out with faggots. These they put to the entrance of the caves and set them on fire. While they were engaged in this business, to their great surprise some of them were desperately wounded with arrows which fell from above on them. This mystery they soon found out. They perceived that the enemy discharged these arrows through holes on the top of the dens directly into the air. Their weight brought them back, point downwards on their enemies heads, whilst they were smoking the inhabitants out. The points of their arrows were poisoned, but their enemy had an antidote for it, which they instantly applied to the wounded part. The smoke at last obliged the people to give themselves up. They came out of their caves, first spatting the palms of their hands together, and immediately after extended their arms, crossed at their wrists, ready to be bound and pinioned. I should judge that the dens above mentioned were extended about eight feet horizontally into the earth, six feet in height and as many wide. They were arched over head and lined with earth, which was of the clay kind, and made the surface of their walls firm and smooth.

The invaders then pinioned the prisoners of all ages and sexes indiscriminately, took their flocks and all their effects, and moved on their way towards the sea. On the march the prisoners were treated with clemency, on account of their being submissive and humble. Having come to the next tribe, the enemy laid siege and immediately took men, women, children, flocks, and all their valuable effects. They then went on to the next district which was contiguous to the sea, called in Africa, Anamaboo. The enemies provisions were then almost spent, as well as their strength. The inhabitants knowing what conduct they had pursued, and what were their present intentions, improved the favorable opportunity, attacked them, and took enemy, prisoners, flocks and all their effects. I was then taken a second time. All of us were then put into the castle, and kept for market. On a certain time I and other prisoners were put on board a canoe, under our master, and rowed away to a vessel belonging to Rhode Island, commanded by Captain Collingwood, and the mate Thomas Mumford. While we were going to the vessel, our master told us all to appear to the best possible advantage for sale. I was bought on board by one Robertson Mumford, steward of said vessel, for four gallons of rum, and a piece of calico, and called VENTURE, on account of his having purchased me with his own private venture. Thus I came by my name. All the slaves that were bought for that vessel's cargo, were two hundred and sixty.

VENTURE SMITH

3

Lydia, the woman whom I have mentioned heretofore, was one of the women whose husbands procured little or nothing for the sustenance of their families, and I often gave her a quarter of a rackoon or a small opossum, for which she appeared very thankful. Her health was not good—she had a bad cough, and often told me she was feverish and restless at night. It appeared clear to me that this woman's constitution was broken by hardships and sufferings, and that she could not live long in her present mode of existence. Her husband, a native of a country far in the interior of Africa, said he had been a priest in his own nation, and had never been taught to do any kind of labor, being supported by the contributions of the public; and he now maintained, as far as he could, the same kind of lazy dignity, that he had enjoyed at home. He was compelled by the overseer to work, with the other hands, in the field, but as soon as he had come into his cabin, he took his seat, and refused to give his wife the least assistance in doing any thing. She was consequently obliged to do the little work that it was necessary to perform in the cabin; and also to bear all the labor of weeding and cultivating the family patch or garden. The husband was a morose, sullen man, and said he formerly had ten wives in his own country, who all had to work for, and wait upon him; and he thought himself badly off here, in having but one woman to do any thing for him. This man was very irritable, and often beat and otherwise maltreated his wife, on the slightest provocation, and the overseer refused to protect her, on the ground, that he never interfered in the family quarrels of the black people. I pitied this woman greatly, but as it was not in my power to remove her from the presence and authority of her husband, I thought it prudent not to say nor do any thing to provoke him further against her. As the winter approached, and the autumnal rains set in, she was frequently exposed in the field, and was wet for several hours together; this, joined to the want of warm and comfortable woollen clothes, caused her to contract colds, and hoarseness, which increased the severity of her cough. A few days before Christmas, her child died, after an illness of only three days. I assisted her and her husband to inter the infant—which was a little boy—and its father buried with it a small bow and several arrows; a little bag of parched meal; a miniature canoe, about a foot long, and a little paddle, (with which he said it would cross the ocean to his own country) a small stick, with an iron nail, sharpened, and fastened into one end of it; and a piece of white muslin, with several curious and strange figures painted on it in blue and red, by which, he said, his relations and countrymen would know the infant to be his son, and would receive it accordingly, on its arrival amongst them.

Cruel as this man was to his wife, I could not but respect the sentiments which inspired his affection for his child; though it was the affection of a barbarian. He cut a lock of hair from his head, threw it upon the dead infant, and closed the grave with his own hands. He then told us the God of his country was looking at him, and was pleased with what he had done. Thus ended the funeral service.

CHARLES BALL

Master and Slave

•··•·•··•··•·•··•·•··•·•··•·•··•·•··•·•··•·•··•·•··•··•

The second CHARLES BALL extract (1836 first edition) gives an overview of conditions and attitudes of the white South. WILLIAM GRIMES, born in Virginia, was the first mulatto slave to have his narrative published. Having escaped to New Haven, he set about getting his narrative published to pay for his freedom since friends of his master, Colonel Thornton, had spied him out (1895 New York edition). FREDERICK DOUGLASS had a meteoric rise as an Abolitionist orator once he had been discovered by William Lloyd Garrison. His narrative had reached a third edition in eighteen months (early 1846 edition). WILLIAM WELLS BROWN rose to prominence when Douglass was under a cloud for agreeing to buy his freedom. Yet Brown did the same eventually. He has the honor of being the first Black American novelist. He wrote *Clotel; or, the President's Daughter* which is partly autobiographical and partly gleaned from then current gossip (1847 edition of the narrative). JOSIAH HENSON, the possible inspiration for Harriet Beecher Stowe's Uncle Tom, had much influence in the settlement of fugitives in Canada. He traveled widely and was presented to Queen Victoria. AUNT CLARA DAVIS's narrative looks back nostalgically from the 1930s to the days of slavery (WPA Project: Alabama narrative).

1

As I advanced southward, even in Virginia, I perceived
that the state of cultivation became progressively
worse. Here, as in Maryland, the practice of the best
farmers who cultivate grain, of planting the land every
alternate year in corn, and sowing it in wheat or rye in
the autumn of the same year in which the corn is
planted, and whilst the corn is yet standing in the field,
so as to get a crop from the same ground every year,
without allowing it time to rest or recover, exhausts
the finest soil in a few years, and in one or two generations reduces the proprietors to poverty. Some, who are
supposed to be very superior farmers, only plant the
land in corn once in three years; sowing it in wheat or
rye as in the former case; however, without any covering of clover or other grass, to protect it from the
rays of the sun. The culture of tobacco prevails over
a large portion of Virginia, especially south of James
River, to the exclusion of almost every other crop,
except corn. This destructive crop ruins the best land
in a short time; and in all the lower parts of Maryland
and Virginia, the traveller will see large old family
mansions of weatherbeaten and neglected appearance,
standing in the middle of vast fields of many hundred
acres, the fences of which have rotted away, and have
been replaced by a wattled work in place of a fence,
composed of short cedar stakes driven into the ground
about two feet apart, and standing about three feet
above the earth; the intervals being filled up by
branches cut from the cedar trees, and worked into the
stakes horizontally after the manner of splits in a
basket.

Many of these fields have been abandoned altogether,
and are overgrown by cedars, which spring up in infinite numbers almost as soon as a field ceases to be

ploughed: and furnish materials for fencing such parts
of the ancient plantation as are still kept enclosed.
In many places, the enclosed fields are only partially
cultivated, all the hills and poorest parts being given
up to the cedars and chinquopin bushes. These estates,
the seats of families that were once powerful, wealthy
and proud, are universally destitute of the appearance
of a barn, such as is known amongst the farmers of
Pennsylvania. The out houses, stables, gardens and of-
fices, have fallen to decay, and the dwelling house is
occupied by the descendants of those who erected it,
still pertinaciously adhering to the halls of their an-
cestry, with a half dozen or ten slaves, the remains
of the two or three hundred who toiled upon these
grounds in former days. The residue of the stock has
been distributed in marriage portions to the daughters
of the family gone to a distance—have been removed
to the west by emigrating sons, or have been sold to the
southern traders, from time to time, to procure money
to support the dignity of the house, as the land grew
poorer, and the tobacco crop shorter, from year to
year.

Industry, enterprise and ambition have fled from
these abodes, and sought refuge from sterility and barrenness in the vales of Kentucky, or the plains of
Alabama; whilst the present occupants, vain of their an-
cestral monuments, and proud of an obscure name,
contend with all the ills that poverty brings upon
fallen greatness, and pass their lives in a contest between mimick state and actual penury—too ignorant
of agriculture, to know how to restore fertility to a
once prolifick and still substantial soil, and too spiritless
to sell their effects and search a new home under other
skies. The sedge grass every where takes possession of
the worn out fields, until it is supplanted by the chinquopin and the cedar. This grass grows in thick set
bunches or stools, and no land is too poor for it. It rises

to the height of two or three feet, and grows, in many places, in great profusion—is utterly worthless, either for hay or pasturage: but affords shelter to numerous rabbits, and countless flocks of partridges; and, at a short distance, has a beautiful appearance, as its elastick, blue tops wave in the breeze.

In Maryland and Virginia, although the slaves are treated with so much rigour, and oftentimes with so much cruelty, I have seen instances of the greatest tenderness of feeling on the part of their owners. I, myself, had three masters in Maryland, and I cannot say now, even after having resided so many years in a state where slavery is not tolerated, that either of them (except the last, who sold me to the Georgians, and was an unfeeling man,) used me worse than they had a moral right to do, regarding me merely as an article of property, and not entitled to any rights as a man, political or civil. My mistresses, in Maryland, were all good women; and the mistress of my wife, in whose kitchen I spent my Sundays and many of my nights, for several years, was a lady of most benevolent and kindly feelings. She was a true friend to me, and I shall always venerate her memory.

It is now my opinion, after all I have seen, that there are no better hearted women in the world, than the ladies of the ancient families, as they are called, in old Virginia, or the country below the mountains, and the same observations will apply to the ladies of Maryland. The stock of slaves has belonged to the family for several generations, and there is a kind of family pride, in being the proprietors of so many human beings, which, in many instances, borders on affection for the people of colour.

If the proprietors of the soil in Maryland and Virginia, were skilful cultivators—had their lands in good condition—and kept no more slaves on each estate, than would be sufficient to work the soil in a proper man-

ner, and keep up the repairs of the place—the condition of the coloured people would not be, by any
means, a comparatively unhappy one. I am convinced,
that in nine cases in ten, the hardships and sufferings
of the coloured population of lower Virginia, are at-
tributable to the poverty and distress of its owners. In
many instances, an estate scarcely yields enough to
feed and clothe the slaves in a comfortable manner,
without allowing any thing for the support of the master and family; but it is obvious, that the family must
first be supported, and the slaves must be content
with the surplus—and this, on a poor, old, worn out
tobacco plantation, is often very small, and wholly
inadequate to the comfortable sustenance of the hands,
as they are called. There, in many places, nothing is
allowed to the poor negro, but his peck of corn
per week, without the sauce of a salt herring, or even a
little salt itself.

Wretched as may be the state of the negroes, in the
quarter, that of the master and his wife and daughters, is, in many instances, not much more enviable in
the old apartments of the *great house*. The sons and
daughters of the family are gentlemen and ladies by
birthright—and were the former to be seen at the
plough, or the latter at the churn or the wash tub, the
honour of the family would be stained, and the dignity
of the house degraded. People must, and will be employed about something, and if they cannot be usefully
occupied, they will most surely engage in some pursuit
wholly unprofitable. So it happens in Virginia—the
young men spend their time in riding about the country, whilst they ought to be ploughing or harrowing in
the cornfield; and the young women are engaged in
reading silly books, or visiting their neighbours houses,
instead of attending to the dairy, or manufacturing
cloth for themselves and their brothers. During all this,
the father is too often defending himself against at-

torneys, or making such terms as he can with the
sheriff, for debts, in which he has been involved by
the vicious idleness of his children, and his own want of
virtue and courage, to break through the evil tyranny
of old customs, and compel his offspring to learn,
in early life, to procure their subsistence by honest and
honourable industry. In this state of things there is not
enough for all. Pride forbids the sale of the slaves,
as long as it is possible to avoid it, and their meagre
allowance of corn is stinted, rather than it shall be said,
the master was obliged to sell them. Somebody must
suffer, and self preservation is the first law of nature,
says the proverb—hunger must invade either the great
house or the quarter, and it is but reasonable to suppose, that so unwelcome an intruder will be expelled,
to the last moment, from the former. In this conflict
of pride and folly, against industry and wisdom, the
slaveholders of Virginia have been unhappily engaged
for more than fifty years.

They are attempting to perform impossibilities—to
draw the means of supporting a life of idleness, luxury,
and splendour, from a once generous, but long since
worn out and exhausted soil—a soil, which, carefully
used, would at this day have richly repaid the toils of
the husbandman, by a noble abundance of all the
comforts of life; but which, tortured into barrenness by
the double curse of slavery and tobacco, stands—and
until its proprietors are regenerated, and learn the difference between a land of slaves and a nation of freemen—must continue to stand, *a monument of the
poverty and punishment which Providence has decreed
as the reward of idleness and tyranny*. The general
features of slavery are the same every where; but the
utmost rigour of the system, is only to be met with, on
the cotton plantations of Carolina and Georgia, or in
the rice fields which skirt the deep swamps and mo-
rasses of the southern rivers. In the tobacco fields of

Maryland and Virginia, great cruelties are practised—
not so frequently by the owners, as by the overseers
of the slaves; but yet, the tasks are not so excessive as
in the cotton region, nor is the press of labour so
incessant throughout the year. It is true, that from the
period when the tobacco plants are set in the field,
there is no resting time until it is housed; but it is
planted out about the first of May, and must be cut
and taken out of the field before the frost comes. After
it is hung and dried, the labour of stripping and preparing it for the hoggshead in leaf, or of manufacturing
it into twist, is comparatively a work of leisure and
ease. Besides, on almost every plantation the hands
are able to complete the work of preparing the tobacco
by January, and sometimes earlier; so that the winter
months, form some sort of respite from the toils of the
year. The people are obliged, it is true, to occupy themselves in cutting wood for the house, making rails and
repairing fences, and in clearing new land, to raise the
tobacco plants for the next year; but as there is usually
time enough, and to spare, for the completion of all
this work, before the season arrives for setting the
plants in the field; the men are seldom flogged much,
unless they are very lazy or negligent, and the women
are allowed to remain in the house, in very cold, snowy,
or rainy weather. I, who am intimately acquainted
with the slavery, both of Maryland and Virginia, and
know that there is no material difference between
the two, ever, that a description of one, is a description
of both; and that the coloured people here have many
advantages over those of the cotton region. There are
seldom more than one hundred, of all ages and conditions, kept on one tobacco plantation; though there are
sometimes many more; but this is not frequent; whilst
on the cotton estates, I have seen four or five hundred, working together in the same vast field. In Maryland, the owners of the estates, generally, reside at

home throughout the year; and the mistress of the mansion is seldom absent more than a few weeks in the winter, when she visits Baltimore or Washington,— the same is the case in Virginia. Her constant residence on the estate, makes her acquainted, personally, with all the slaves, and she frequently interests herself in their welfare, often interceding with the master, her husband, to prevent the overseer from beating them unmercifully.

The young ladies of the family also, if there be any, after they have left school, are generally at home until they are married. Each of them universally claims a young black girl as her own, and takes her under her protection. This enables the girl to extend the protection and friendship of *young mistress* to her father, mother, brothers and sisters. The sons of the family likewise, have their favourites among the black boys, and have many disputes with the *overseer* if he abuses them. All these advantages accrue to the black people, from the circumstance of the master and his family living at home. In Maryland I never knew a mistress, or a young mistress, who would not listen to the complaints of the slaves. It is true, we were always obliged to approach the door of the mansion, in the most humble and supplicating manner, with our hats in our hands, and the most subdued and beseeching language in our mouths—but, in return, we generally received words of kindness, and very often a redress of our grievances; though I have known very great ladies, who would never grant any request from the *plantation hands*, but always referred them and their petitions to their master, under a pretence, that they could not meddle with things that did not belong to the house. The mistresses of the great families, generally gave mild language to the slaves; though they sometimes sent for the overseer and had them severely flogged; but I have never heard any mistress, in either

Maryland or Virginia, indulge in the low, vulgar and profane vituperations, of which I was myself the object, in Georgia, for several years, whenever I came into the presence of my mistress. Flogging—though often severe and excruciating in Maryland, is not practised with the order, regularity and system, to which it is reduced in the South. On the Potomack, if a slave gives offence, he is generally chastised on the spot, in the field where he is at work, as the overseer always carries a whip—sometimes a twisted cow-hide, sometimes a kind of horse-whip, and very often a simple hickory switch or gad, cut in the adjoining woods. For stealing meat, or other provisions, or for any of the *higher* offences, the slaves are stripped, tied up by the hands—sometimes by the thumbs—and whipped at the quarter—but, many times, on a large tobacco plantation, there is not more than one of these regular whippings in a week—though on others, where the master happens to be a bad man, or a drunkard—the back of the unhappy Maryland slave, is seamed with scars from his neck to his hips.

CHARLES BALL

2

I then started with my new master for Savannah, with a carriage and four horses: we travelled about twelve miles the first day. I was dissatisfied with him before I had got two miles. We travelled the next day twenty-five miles, as far as Petersburgh. I was so much dissatisfied with him, that I offered a black man at that place, two silver dollars to take an axe and break my leg, in order that I could not go on to Savannah; but he refused, saying he could tell me a better way. I asked him how? He said runaway. I told him I would not run away unless I was sure of gaining my freedom by doing it. We then travelled on the next day about thirty miles, and put up for the night. I then attempted to break my leg myself. Accordingly I took up an axe, and laying my leg on a log, I struck at it several times with an axe endeavouring to break it, at the same time I put up my fervent prayers to God to be my guide, saying, "if it be thy will that I break my leg in order that I may not go on to Georgia, grant that my blows may take effect; but thy will not mine be done." Finding I could not hit my leg after a number of fruitless attempts, I was convinced by my feelings then, that God had not left me in my sixth trouble, and would be with me in the seventh. Accordingly I tried no more to destroy myself. I then prayed to God, that if it was his will that I should go, that I might willingly. My old master and mistress in Virginia, had often threatened to sell me to the negro buyer from Georgia for any trifling offence, and in order to make me dislike to go there, they would tell me I should have to eat cotton seed, and make indigo, and not have corn bread to eat as I did in Virginia. The next day we went as far as Columbia, in South Carolina. This was Saturday evening.

I was quite fatigued, and after taking care of the horses, I laid myself down in the stable to rest. I soon fell asleep, and slept for an hour or two. My master missing me, and thinking I had run away, made a thorough search for me, but could not find me until I awoke and went into the house. He was very angry with me: he cursed me and asked me where I had been. I told him I had been asleep in the stable. He told me I lied, and that I had attempted to make my escape; threatening to whip me. I told him I had not attempted any thing of the kind; but he would not believe me. Here again I was in great trouble. I went to bed and slept as well as I could, which was but little. The next day we again pursued our journey, and noth-

ing of any consequence, different from what had before taken place, until we arrived at Savannah, which
was in about six weeks. As we entered the city, we
were about to pass a man who had a gun on his shoulder, loaded with shot. It accidentally went off, the
contents within a very few inches of me. Here again,
I escaped a wound, if not death. After residing in
Savannah for a few months, and perceiving that he
grew more severe and inhuman with me every day I
began to despair of ever living with him in peace. I
however found some friends in Savannah, after a short
time, and they advised me (after being made acquainted with the manner in which I was used) to get
away from him as soon as possible. He would never
allow me to leave the yard, unless it was for the purpose of taking out his horses to exercise them. At
such times, I would often go to the fortune-teller,
and by paying her twenty-five cents, she would tell
me what she said my fortune would be. She told me
I should eventually get away, but that it would be attended with a great deal of trouble; and truly, I experienced a vast deal of trouble before I could get
away.

WILLIAM GRIMES

3

If at any one time of my life more than another, I was
made to drink the bitterest dregs of slavery, that time
was during the first six months of my stay with Mr.
Covey. We were worked in all weathers. It was never
too hot or too cold; it could never rain, blow, hail, or
snow too hard for us to work in the field. Work, work,
work was scarcely more the order of the day than of
the night. The longest days were too short for him, and
the shortest nights too long for him. I was somewhat

unmanageable when I first went there, but a few months of this discipline tamed me. Mr. Covey succeeded in breaking me. I was broken in body, soul, and spirit. My natural elasticity was crushed, my intellect languished, the disposition to read departed, the cheerful spark that lingered about my eye died; the dark night of slavery closed in upon me; and behold a man transformed into a brute!

Sunday was my only leisure time. I spent this in a sort of beast-like stupor, between sleep and wake, under some large tree. At times I would rise up, a flash of energetic freedom would dart through my soul, accompanied with a faint gleam of hope, that flickered for a moment, and then vanished. I sank down again, mourning over my wretched condition. I was sometimes prompted to take my life, and that of Covey, but was prevented by a combination of hope and fear. My sufferings on this plantation seem now like a dream rather than a stern reality.

Our house stood within a few rods of the Chesapeake Bay, whose broad bosom was ever white with sails from every quarter of the habitable globe. Those beautiful vessels robed in purest white, so delightful to the eye of freemen, were to me so many shrouded ghosts, to terrify and torment me with thoughts of my wretched condition. I have often, in the deep stillness of a summer's Sabbath, stood all alone upon the lofty banks of that noble bay, and traced, with saddened heart and tearful eye, the countless number of sails moving off to the mighty ocean. The sight of these always affected me powerfully. My thoughts would compel utterance; and there, with no audience but the Almighty, I would pour out my soul's complaint, in my rude way, with an apostrophe to the moving multitude of ships:—

"You are loosed from your moorings, and are free; I am fast in my chains, and am a slave! You move

merrily before the gentle gale, and I sadly before
the bloody whip! You are freedom's swift-winged an-
gels, that fly round the world; I am confined in bands
of iron! O that I were free! O, that I were on one of
your gallant decks, and under your protecting wing!
Alas! betwixt me and you the turbid waters roll. Go
on, go on. O that I could also go! Could I but swim!
If I could fly! O, why was I born a man, of whom to
make a brute! The glad ship is gone; she hides in the
dim distance. I am left in the hottest hell of unending
slavery. O God, save me! God, deliver me! Let me be
free! Is there any God? Why am I a slave? I will run
away. I will not stand it. Get caught or get clear, I'll
try it. I had as well die with ague as the fever. I have
only one life to lose. I had as well be killed running
as die standing. Only think of it; one hundred miles
straight north, and I am free! Try it? Yes! God helping me, I will. It cannot be that I shall live and die a
slave. I will take to the water. This very bay shall yet
bear me into freedom. The steamboats steered in a
north-east course from North Point. I will do the same;
and when I go to the head of the bay, I will turn my
canoe adrift, and walk straight through Delaware into
Pennsylvania. When I get there, I shall not be required to have a pass; I can travel without being
disturbed. Let but the first opportunity offer, and come
what will, I am off. Meanwhile, I will try to bear up
under the yoke. I am not the only slave in the world.
Why should I fret? I can bear as much as any of
them. Besides, I am but a boy, and all boys are bound
to some one. It may be that my misery in slavery will
only increase my happiness when I get free. There is
a better day coming.

Thus I used to think, and thus I used to speak to
myself; goaded almost to madness at one moment, and
at the next reconciling myself to my wretched lot.

I have already intimated that my condition was

much worse during the first six months of my stay at Mr. Covey's, than in the last six. The circumstances leading to the change in Mr. Covey's course toward me form an epoch in my humble history. You have seen how man was made a slave; you shall see how a slave was made a man. On one of the hottest days of the month of August, 1833, Bill Smith, William Hughes, a slave named Eli, and myself were engaged in fanning wheat. Hughes was clearing the fanned wheat from before the fan, Eli was turning, Smith was feeding, and I was carrying wheat to the fan. The work was simple, requiring strength rather than intellect; yet, to one entirely unused to such work, it came very hard. About three o'clock of that day, I broke down; my strength failed me; I was seized with a violent aching of the head, attended with extreme dizziness; I trembled in every limb. Finding what was coming, I nerved myself up, feeling it would never do to stop work. I stood as long as I could stagger to the hopper with grain. When I could stand no longer, I fell, and felt as if held down by some immense weight. The fan of course stopped; every one had his own work to do; and no one could do the work of the other, and have his own go on at the same time.

Mr. Covey was at the house, about one hundred yards from the treading-yard where we were fanning. On hearing the fan stop, he left immediately, and came to the spot where we were. He hastily enquired what the matter was. Bill answered that I was sick, and there was no one to bring wheat to the fan. I had by this time crawled away under the side of the post and rail-fence by which the yard was enclosed, hoping to find relief by getting out of the sun. He then asked where I was. He was told by one of the hands. He came to the spot, and after looking at me awhile, asked me what was the matter. I told him as well as I could, for I scarce had strength to speak. He then gave me a savage kick in the side, and told me to get up. I tried to do so, but fell back in the attempt. He gave me another kick, and again told me to rise. I again tried, and succeeded in gaining my feet: but, stooping to get the tub with which I was feeding the fan, I again staggered and fell. While down in this situation, Mr. Covey took up the hickory slat with which Hughes had been striking off the half-bushel measure, and with it gave me a heavy blow upon the head, making a large wound, and the blood ran freely; and with this, again told me to get up. I made no effort to comply, having now made up my mind to let him do his worst. In a short time after receiving this blow, my head grew better. Mr. Covey had now left me to my fate. At this moment I resolved, for the first time, to go to my master, enter a complaint, and ask his protection. In order to this, I must that afternoon walk seven miles; and this, under the circumstances, was truly a severe undertaking. I was exceedingly feeble; made so as much by the kicks and blows which I received, as by the severe fit of sickness to which I had been subjected. I, however, watched my chance, while Covey was looking in an opposite direction, and started for St. Michael's. I succeeded in getting a considerable distance on my way to the woods, when Covey discovered me, and called after me to come back, threatening what he would do if I did not come. I disregarded both his calls and his threats, and made my way to the woods as fast as my feeble state would allow; and thinking I might be overhauled by him if I kept the road, I walked through the woods, keeping far enough from the road to avoid detection, and near enough to prevent losing my way. I had not gone far, before my little strength again failed me. I could go no farther. I fell down, and lay for a considerable time. The blood was yet oozing from the wound on my head. For a time I thought I should bleed to death, and think now that I should have done so, but that the blood so matted my hair as to stop the wound. After lying there about three quarters of an hour, I nerved myself up again, and started on my way, through bogs and briers, barefooted and bareheaded, tearing my feet sometimes at nearly every step; and after a journey of about seven miles, occupying some five hours to perform it, I arrived at master's store. I then presented an appearance enough to affect any but a heart of iron. From the crown of my head to my feet, I was covered with blood. My hair was all clotted with dust and blood; my shirt was stiff with blood. My legs and feet were torn in sundry places with briers and thorns, and were also covered with blood. I suppose I looked like a man who had escaped a den of wild beasts, and barely escaped them. In this state I appeared before my master, humbly entreating him to interpose his authority for my protection. I told him all the circumstances as well as I could, and it seemed, as I spoke, at times to affect him. He would then walk the floor, and seek to justify Covey by saying he expected I deserved it. He asked me what I wanted. I told him to let me get a new home; that as sure as I lived with Mr. Covey again, I should live with but to die with him; that Covey would surely kill me—he was in a fair way for it. Master Thomas ridiculed the idea that there was any danger of Mr. Covey's killing me, and said that he knew Mr. Covey; that he was a good man, and that he could not think of taking me from him; that should he do so, he would lose the whole year's wages; that I belonged to Mr. Covey for one year, and that I must go back to him, come what might; and that I must not trouble him with any more stories, or that he would himself *get hold of me*. After threatening me thus, he gave me a very large dose of salts, telling me that I might remain in St. Machael's that night, (it being quite late,) but that I must be off

back to Mr. Covey's early in the morning; and that if
I did not, he would *get hold of me*, which meant that
he would whip me. I remained all night, and according
to his orders, I started off to Covey's in the morning,
(Saturday morning) wearied in body and broken in
spirit. I got no supper that night, or breakfast that
morning. I reached Covey's about nine o'clock; and
just as I was getting over the fence that divided Mrs.
Kemp's fields from ours, out ran Covey with his cow-
skin, to give me another whipping. Before he could
reach me, I succeeded in getting to the cornfield; and
as the corn was very high, it afforded me the means
of hiding. He seemed very angry, and searched for me
a long time. My behaviour was altogether unaccountable. He finally gave up the chase, thinking, I suppose,
that I must come home for something to eat; he would
give himself no further trouble in looking for me. I
spent that day mostly in the woods, having the alterna-
tive before me,—to go home and be whipped to death,
or stay in the woods and be starved to death. That
night, I fell in with Sandy Jenkins, a slave with whom
I was somewhat acquainted. Sandy had a free wife,
who lived about four miles from Mr. Covey's; and it
being Saturday, he was on his way to see her. I told
him my circumstances, and he very kindly invited me
to go home with him. I went home with him, and
talked this whole matter over, and got his advice as to
what course it was best for me to pursue. I found Sandy
an old adviser. He told me, with great solemnity, I
must go back to Covey; but that before I went, I
must go with him into another part of the woods,
where there was a certain *root*, which, if I would take
some of it with me, carrying it *always on my right side*,
would render it impossible for Mr. Covey, or any other
white man, to whip me. He said he had carried it for
years; and since he had done so, he had never received
a blow, and never expected to, while he carried it. I at

first rejected the idea, that the simple carrying of a
root in my pocket would have any such effect as he
had said, and was not disposed to take it; but Sandy
impressed the necessity with much earnestness, telling
me it could do no harm, if it did no good. To please
him, I at length took the *root*, and, according to his
direction, carried it upon my right side. This was Sunday morning. I immediately started for home; and
upon entering the yard gate, out came Mr. Covey on
his way to meeting. He spoke to me very kindly, bade
me drive the pigs from a lot near by, and passed on
towards the church. Now this singular conduct of Mr.
Covey really made me begin to think that there was
something in the *root* which Sandy had given me; and
had it been on any other day than Sunday, I could
have attributed the conduct to no other cause than the
influence of that *root*; and as it was, I was half inclined to think the *root* to be something more than I
at first had taken it to be. All went well till Monday
morning. On this morning, the virtue of the *root* was
fully tested. Long before daylight, I was called to go
and rub, curry, and feed the horses. I obeyed, and was
glad to obey. But whilst thus engaged, whilst in the
act of throwing down some blades from the loft, Mr.
Covey entered the stable with a long rope; and just
as I was half out of the loft, he caught hold of my
legs, and was about tying me. As soon as I found what
he was up to, I gave a sudden spring, and as I did so,
he holding to my legs, I was brought sprawling on the
stable floor. Mr. Covey seemed now to think he had
me, and could do what he pleased; but at this moment
—from whence came the spirit I don't know—I resolved to fight; and suiting my action to the resolution,
I seized Covey hard by the throat; and as I did so, I
rose. He held on to me, and I to him. My resistance
was so entirely unexpected, that Covey seemed taken
all aback. He trembled like a leaf. This gave me assurance, and I held him uneasy, causing the blood to

run where I touched him with the ends of my fingers. Mr. Covey soon called out to Hughes for help. Hughes came, and, while Covey held me, attempted to tie my right hand. While he was in the act of doing so, I watched my chance, and gave him a heavy kick close under the ribs. This kick fairly sickened Hughes, so that he left me in the hands of Mr. Covey. This kick had the effect of not only weakening Hughes, but Covey also. When he saw Hughes bending over with pain, his courage quailed. He asked me if I meant to persist in my resistance. I told him I did, come what might; that he had used me like a brute for six months, and that I was determined to be used so no longer. With that, he strove to drag me to a stick that was lying just out of the stable door. He meant to knock me down. But just as he was leaning over to get the stick, I seized him with both hands by his collar, and brought him by a sudden snatch to the ground. By this time, Bill came. Covey called upon him for assistance. Bill wanted to know what he could do. Covey said, "Take hold of him, take hold of him!" Bill said his master hired him out to work, and not to help to whip me; so he left Covey and myself to fight our own battle out. We were at it for nearly two hours. Covey at length let me go, puffing and blowing at a great rate, saying that if I had not resisted, he would not have whipped me half so much. The truth was, that he had not whipped me at all. I considered him as getting entirely the worst end of the bargain; for he had drawn no blood from me, but I had from him. The whole six months afterwards, that I spent with Mr. Covey, he never laid the weight of his finger upon me in anger. He would occasionally say, he didn't want to get hold of me again. "No," thought I, "you need not; for you will come off worse than you did before."

This battle with Mr. Covey was the turning-point in my career as a slave. It rekindled the few expiring embers of freedom, and revived within me a sense of my own manhood. It recalled the departed self-confidence, and inspired me again with a determination to be free. The gratification afforded by the triumph was a full compensation for whatever else might follow, even death itself. He only can understand the deep satisfaction which I experienced, who has himself repelled by force the bloody arm of slavery. I felt as I never felt before. It was a glorious resurrection from the tomb of slavery to the heaven of freedom. My long-crushed spirit rose, cowardice departed, bold defiance took its place; and I now resolved that, however long I might remain a slave in form, the day had passed forever when I could be a slave in fact. I did not hesitate to let it be known of me, that the white man who expected to succeed in whipping, must also succeed in killing me.

From this time I was never again what might be called fairly whipped, though I remained a slave four years afterwards. I had several fights, but was never whipped.

It was for a long time a matter of surprise to me, why Mr. Covey did not immediately have me taken by the constable to the whipping-post, and there regularly whipped for the crime of raising my hand against a white man in defence of myself. And the only explanation I can now think of does not entirely satisfy me; but such as it is, I will give it. Mr. Covey enjoyed the most unbounded reputation for being a first-rate overseer and negro-breaker. It was of considerable importance to him. That reputation was at stake; and had he sent me—a boy about sixteen years old—to the public whipping-post, his reputation would have been lost; so, to save his reputation, he suffered me to go unpunished.

My term of actual service to Mr. Edward Covey ended on Christmas day, 1833.

FREDERICK DOUGLASS

4

Soon after this, I was hired out to Mr. Walker; the same man whom I have mentioned as having carried a gang of slaves down the river, on the steamboat *Enterprize*. Seeing me in the capacity of steward on the boat, and thinking that I would make a good hand to take care of slaves, he determined to have me for that purpose; and finding that my master would not sell me, he hired me for the term of one year.

When I learned the fact of my having been hired to a negro speculator, or a "soul-driver" as they are generally called among slaves, no one can tell my emotions. Mr. Walker had offered a high price for me, as I afterwards learned, but I suppose my master was restrained from selling me by the fact that I was a near relative of his. On entering the service of Mr. Walker, I found that my opportunity of getting to a land of liberty was gone, at least for the time being. He had a gang of slaves in readiness to start for New Orleans, and in a few days we were on our journey. I am at a loss for language to express my feelings on that occasion. Although my master had told me that he had not sold me, and Mr. Walker had told me that he had not purchased me, I did not believe them; and not until I had been to New Orleans, and was on my return, did I believe that I was not sold.

There was on the boat a large room on the lower deck, in which the slaves were kept, men and women, promiscuously—all chained two and two, and a strict watch kept that they did not get loose; for cases have occurred in which slaves have got off their chains, and made their escape at landing-places, while the boats were taking in wood;—and with all our care, we lost one woman who had been taken from her husband and children, and having no desire to live without them, in the agony of her soul jumped overboard, and drowned herself. She was not chained.

It was almost impossible to keep that part of the boat clean.

On landing at Natchez, the slaves were all carried to the slave-pen, and there kept one week, during which time, several of them were sold. Mr. Walker fed his slaves well. We took on board, at St. Louis, several hundred pounds of bacon (smoked meat) and corn-meal, and his slaves were better fed than slaves generally were in Natchez, so far as my observation extended.

At the end of a week, we left for New Orleans, the place of our final destination, which we reached in two days. Here the slaves were placed in a negro-pen, where those who wished to purchase could call and examine them. The negro-pen is a small yard, surrounded by buildings, from fifteen to twenty feet wide, with the exception of a large gate with iron bars. The slaves are kept in the buildings during the night, and turned out into the yard during the day. After the best of the stock was sold at private sale at the pen, the balance were taken to the Exchange Coffee House Auction Rooms, kept by Isaac L. McCoy, and sold at public auction. After the sale of this lot of slaves, we left New Orleans for St. Louis.

On our arrival at St. Louis, I went to Dr. Young, and told him that I did not wish to live with Mr. Walker any longer. I was heart-sick at seeing my fellow-creatures bought and sold. But the Dr. had hired me for the year, and stay I must. Mr. Walker again commenced purchasing another gang of slaves. He bought a man of Colonel John O'Fallon, who resided in the suburbs of the city. This man had a wife and three children. As soon as the purchase was made, he was put in jail for safekeeping, until we should be ready to start for New Orleans. His wife visited him while there, several times, and several times when she went for that purpose was refused admittance.

In the course of eight or nine weeks Mr. Walker had his cargo of human flesh made up. There was in this lot a number of old men and women, some of them with gray locks. We left St. Louis in the steamboat *Carlton*, Captain Swan, bound for New Orleans. On our way down, and before we reached Rodney, the place where we made our first stop, I had to prepare the old slaves for market. I was ordered to have the old men's whiskers shaved off, and the grey hairs plucked out, where they were not too numerous, in which case he had a preparation of blacking to color it, and with a blacking-brush we would put it on. This was new business to me, and was performed in a room where the passengers could not see us. These slaves were also taught how old they were by Mr. Walker, and after going through the blacking process, they looked ten or fifteen years younger; and I am sure that some of those who purchased slaves of Mr. Walker, were dreadfully cheated, especially in the ages of the slaves which they bought.

We landed at Rodney, and the slaves were driven to the pen in the back part of the village. Several were sold at this place, during our stay of four or five days, when we proceeded to Natchez. There we landed at night, and the gang were put in the warehouse until morning, when they were driven to the pen. As soon as the slaves are put in these pens, swarms of planters may be seen in and about them. They knew when Walker was expected, as he always had the time advertised beforehand when he would be in Rodney, Natchez, and New Orleans. These were the principal places where he offered his slaves for sale.

When at Natchez the second time, I saw a slave very cruelly whipped. He belonged to a Mr. Broadwell, a merchant who kept a store on the wharf. The slave's name was Lewis. I had known him several years, as he was formerly from St. Louis. We were expecting a steamboat down the river, in which we were to take passage for New Orleans. Mr. Walker sent me to the landing to watch for the boat, ordering me to inform him on its arrival. While there, I went into the store to see Lewis. I saw a slave in the store, and asked him where Lewis was. Said he, "They have got Lewis hanging between the heavens and the earth." I asked him what he meant by that. He told me to go into the warehouse and see. I went in, and found Lewis there. He was tied up to a beam, with his toes just touching the floor. As there was no one in the warehouse but himself, I inquired the reason of his being in that situation. He said Mr. Broadwell had sold his wife to a planter six miles from the city, and that he had been to visit her,—that he went in the night, expecting to return before daylight, and went without his master's permission. The patrol had taken him up before he reached his wife. He was put in jail, and his master had to pay for his catching and keeping, and that was what he was tied up for.

Just as he finished his story, Mr. Broadwell came in, and inquired what I was doing there. I knew not what to say, and while I was thinking what reply to make, he struck me over the head with the cowhide, the end of which struck me over my right eye, sinking deep into the flesh, leaving a scar which I carry to this day. Before I visited Lewis, he had received fifty lashes. Mr. Broadwell gave him fifty lashes more after I came out, as I was afterwards informed by Lewis himself.

The next day we proceeded to New Orleans, and put the gang in the same negro-pen which we occupied before. In a short time, the planters came flocking to the pen to purchase slaves. Before the slaves were exhibited for sale, they were dressed and driven out into the yard. Some were set to dancing, some to jumping, some to singing, and some to playing cards. This was done to make them appear cheerful and happy. My business was to see that they were placed in those situations before the arrival of the purchasers, and I have often set them to dancing when their cheeks were wet with tears. As slaves were in good demand at that time, they were all soon disposed of, and we again set out for St. Louis.

WILLIAM WELLS BROWN

5

On one of these occasions my master got into a quarrel with his brother's overseer, Bryce Litton. All present sided with Litton against him, and soon there was a general row. I was sitting, at the time, out on the front steps of the tavern, and, hearing the scuffle, rushed in to look after my charge. My master, a stout man and a terrible bruiser, could generally hold his own in an ordinary general fight, and clear a handsome space around him; but now he was cornered, and a dozen were striking at him with fists, crockery, chairs, and anything that came handy. The moment he saw me he hallooed, "That's it, Sie! pitch in! show me fair play." It was a rough business, and I went in roughly, shoving, tripping, and doing my best for the rescue. With infinite trouble, and many a bruise on my own head and shoulders, I at length got him out of the room. He was crazy with drink and rage, and struggled hard with me to get back and renew the fight. But I managed to force him into his wagon, jump in, and drive off.

By ill-luck, in the height of the scuffle, Bryce Litton got a severe fall. Whether the whisky he had drunk, or a chance shove from me, was the cause, I am unable to say. He, however, attributed it to me, and treasured up his vengeance for the first favorable opportunity. The opportunity soon came.

About a week afterwards I was sent by my master to a place a few miles distant, on horseback, with some letters. I took a short cut through a lane, separated by gates from the high road, and bounded by a fence on each side. This lane passed through some of the farm owned by my master's brother, and his overseer was in the adjoining field, with three negroes, when I went by. On my return, half an hour afterwards, the overseer was sitting on the fence; but I could see nothing of the black fellows. I rode on, utterly unsuspicious of any trouble; but as I approached he jumped off the fence, and at the same moment two of the negroes sprang up from under the bushes where they had been concealed, and stood with him immediately in front of me, while the third sprang over the fence just behind me. I was thus enclosed between what I could no longer doubt were hostile forces. The overseer seized my horse's bridle, and ordered me to alight, in the usual elegant phraseology addressed by such men to slaves. I asked what I was to alight for. "To take the cursedest flogging you ever had in your life, you d—d black scoundrel." "But what am I to be flogged for, Mr. L.?" I asked. "Not a word," said he, "but 'light at once, and take off your jacket." I saw there was nothing else to be done, and slipped off the horse on the opposite side from him. "Now take off your shirt," cried he; and as I demurred at this, he lifted a stick he had in his hand to strike me, but so suddenly and violently that he frightened the horse, which broke away from him and ran home. I was thus left without means of escape, to sustain the attacks of four men, as well as I might. In avoiding Mr. L.'s blow, I had accidentally got into a corner of the fence, where I could not be approached except in front. The overseer called upon the negroes to seize me; but they, knowing something of my physical power, were rather slow to obey. At length they did their best, and as they brought themselves within my reach, I knocked them down successively; and one of them trying to trip up my feet when he was down, I gave him a kick with my heavy shoe, which knocked out several teeth, and sent him howling away.

Meanwhile Bryce Litton played away on my head with a stick, not heavy enough, indeed, to knock me down, but drawing blood freely; shouting all the while, "Won't you give up! won't you give up! you black son of a bitch!" Exasperated at my defence, he suddenly seized a heavy fence-rail, and rushed at me to bring matters to a sudden close. The ponderous blow fell; I lifted my arm to ward it off; the bone cracked like a pipe-stem, and I fell headlong to the ground. Repeated blows then rained on my back, till both shoulder-blades were broken, and the blood gushed copiously from my mouth. In vain the negroes interposed. "Didn't you see the damned nigger strike me?" Of course they must say "yes," although the lying coward had avoided close quarters, and fought with his stick alone. At length, his vengeance satisfied, he desisted, telling me to learn what it was to strike a white man.

Meanwhile an alarm had been raised at the house by the return of the horse without his rider, and my master started off with a small party to learn what the trouble was. When he first saw me he was swearing with rage. "You've been fighting, you damned nigger!" I told him Bryce Litton had been beating me, because I shoved him the other night at the tavern, when they had a fuss. Seeing how much I was injured, he became still more fearfully mad; and after having me carried home, mounted his horse and rode over to Montgomery Court House, to enter a complaint. Little good came of it. Litton swore that when he spoke to me in the lane, I "sassed" him, jumped off my horse and made at him, and would have killed him but for the help of his negroes. Of course no negro's testimony could be admitted against a white man, and he was acquitted. My master was obliged to pay all the costs of court; and although he had the satisfaction of calling Litton a liar and scoundrel, and giving him a tremendous bruising, still even this partial compensation was rendered less gratifying by what followed, which was a suit for damages and a heavy fine.

My sufferings after this cruel treatment were intense. Besides my broken arm and the wounds on my head, I could feel and hear the pieces of my shoulder-blades grate against each other with every breath. No physician or surgeon was called to dress my wounds; and I never knew one to be called on Riley's estate on any occasion whatever. "A nigger will get well anyway," was a fixed principle of faith, and facts seemed to justify it. The robust, physical health produced by a life of out-door labor, made our wounds heal up with as little inflammation as they do in the case of cattle. I was attended by my master's sister, Miss Patty, as we called her, the Esculapius of the plantation. She was a powerful, big-boned woman, who flinched at no responsibility, from wrenching out teeth to setting bones. I have seen her go into the house and get a rifle to shoot a furious ox that the negroes were in vain trying to butcher. She splintered my arm and bound up my back as well as she knew how. Alas! it was but cobbler's work. From that day to this I have been unable to raise my hands as high as my head. It was five months before I could work at all, and the first time I tried to plough, a hard knock of the colter against a stone shattered my shoulderblades again, and gave me even greater agony than at first. And so I have gone through life maimed and mutilated. Practice in time enabled me to perform many of the farm labors with considerable efficiency; but the free, vigorous play of muscle and arm was gone forever.

JOSIAH HENSON

6

"I was bawn in de year 1845, white folks," said Aunt Clara, "on de Mosley plantation in Bellvy jus' nawth of Monroeville. Us had a mighty pretty place back dar. Massa Mosely had near 'bout five hundred acres an' mos' near to one hundred slaves.

"Was Marse Mosely good to us? Lor', honey, how you talk. Co'se he was! He was de bes' white man in de lan'. Us had eve'y thing dat we could hope to eat: turkey, chicken, beef, lamb, poke, vegetables, fruits, aigs, butter, milk. . . . we jus' had eve'ything, white folks, eve'ything. Dem was de good ole days. How I longs to be back dar wid my ole folks an' a playin' wid de chilluns down by de creek. 'Tain't nothin' lak it today, nawsuh. When I tell you 'bout it you gwine to wish you was dar too.

"White folks, you can have your automobiles an' paved streets an' electric lights. I don't want 'em. You can have de busses an' street cars an' hot pavements an' high buildin' 'caze I ain't got no use for 'em no way. But I'll tell you what I does want. I wants my ole cotton bed an' de moonlight nights a shinin' through de willow trees an' de cool grass under my feets as I runned aroun' ketchin' lightnin' bugs. I wants to hear de sound of de hounds in de woods atter de 'possum, an' de smell of fresh mowed hay. I wants to feel de sway of de ol' wagon a-goin' down de red, dusty road an' listen to de wheels groanin' as dey rolls along. I wants to sink my teeth into some of dat good ol' ash cake, an' smack de good ol' sorghum offen my mouth.

White folks I wants to see de boats a passin' up an' down de Alabamy ribber an' hear de slaves a singin' at dere work. I wants to see de dawn break over de black ridge an' de twilight settle over de place spreadin' a sort of orange hue over de place. I wants to walk de paths th'ew de woods an' see de rabbits an' watch de birds an' listen to frogs at night. But dey tuk me away f'om dat a long time ago. 'Twarn't long befo' I ma'ied an' had chilluns, but don't none of 'em 'tribute to my suppote now. One of 'em was killed in de big war wid Germany and de res' is all scattered out . . . eight of 'em. Now I jus' live f'om han' to mouth; here one day, somewhere else de nex'. I guess we's all a-goin' to die iffen dis 'pression don't let us 'lone. Maybe someday I'll get to go home. Dey tells me dat when a pusson crosses dat ribber, de Lawd gives him whut he wants. I done tol' de Lawd I don't want nothin' much . . . only my home, white folks. I don't think dats much to ax for. I suppose he'll sen' me back dar. I been a-waitin' for him to call."

AUNT CLARA SMITH

Slaveholder Brutality

•··•··•··•··•··•··•··•··•··•··•··•··•··•··•··•

JOHN BROWN's narrative was heavily edited by his sponsor yet the extract shows plenty of personal vigor (1855 edition of *Slave Life in Georgia*). MOSES ROPER had his narrative of fifty-one pages first published in London in 1837. By 1840, and with three more editions, the same narrative had reached one hundred pages. His sponsors considered him an "excellent young man" whose education could be furthered by proceeds from the narrative (1846 Berwick-on-Tweed edition). SOLOMON NORTHUP had the misfortune to be kidnapped into slavery after being born free. His narrative vividly recalls his nine years with Mr. Edwin Epps, the cotton owner of Bayou Boeuf, Louisiana (1853 edition, dedicated to Mrs. Beecher Stowe).

1

I had been fourteen years with Stevens, suffering all the time very much from his ill-treatment of me, when he fell ill. I do not know what his malady was. It must have been serious, for they called in to treat him one Doctor Hamilton, who lived in Jones County, and who had a great name. He cured Stevens, who was so pleased, that he told the Doctor to ask him any favour, and it should be granted. Now it so happened that this Doctor Hamilton had been trying a great number of experiments, for the purpose of finding out the best remedies for sun-stroke. I was, it seems, a strong and likely subject to be experimented upon, and the Doctor having fixed the thing in his mind, asked Stevens to lend me to him. This he did at once, never caring to inquire what was going to be done with me. I myself did not know. Even if I had been made aware of the nature of the trials I was about to undergo, I could not have helped myself. There was nothing for it but passive resignation, and I gave myself up in ignorance and in much fear.

Yet, it was not without curiosity I watched the progress of the preparations the Doctor caused to be made. He ordered a hole to be dug in the ground, three feet and a half deep by three feet long, and two feet and a half wide. Into this pit a quantity of dried red oak bark was cast, and fire set to it. It was allowed to burn until the pit became heated like an oven, when the embers were taken out. A plank was then put across the bottom of the pit, and on that a stool. Having tested, with a thermometer, the degree to which the pit was heated, the Doctor bade me strip, and get in; which I did, only my head being above the ground. He then gave me some medicine which he had prepared, and as soon as I was on the stool, a number of wet blankets were fastened over the hole, and scantlings laid across them. This was to keep in the heat. It soon began to tell upon me; but though I tried hard to keep up against its effects, in about half an hour I fainted. I was then lifted out and revived, the Doctor taking a note of the degree of heat when

I left the pit. I used to be put in between daylight and dark, after I had done my day's work; for Stevens was not a man to lose more of the labour of his slaves than he could help. Three or four days afterwards, the experiment was repeated, and so on for five or six times, the Doctor allowing me a few days' rest between each trial. His object was to ascertain which of the medicines he administered to me on these occasions, enabled me to withstand the greatest degree of heat. He found that cayenne-pepper tea accomplished this object; and a very nice thing he made of it. As soon as he got back home, he advertised that he had discovered a remedy for sun-stroke. It consisted of pills, which were to be dissolved in a dose of cayenne-pepper tea, without which, he said, the pills would not produce any effect. Nor do I see how they should have done so, for they were only made of common flour. However, he succeeded in getting them into general use, and as he asked a good price, he soon realized a large fortune.

Having completed his series of experiments upon me, in the heated pit, and allowed me some days' rest, I was put on a diet, and then, during a period of about three weeks, he bled me every other day. At the end of that time he found I was failing, so he left off, and I got a month's rest, to regain a little strength. At the expiration of that time, he set to work to ascertain how deep my black skin went. This he did by applying blisters to my hands, legs and feet, which bear the scars to this day. He continued until he drew up the dark skin from between the upper and the under one. He used to blister me at intervals of about two weeks. He also tried other experiments upon me, which I cannot dwell upon.

Altogether, and from first to last, I was in his hands, under treatment, for about nine months, at the end of which period I had become so weak, that I was no

longer able to work in the fields. I had never been allowed to knock off, I ought to say, during the whole
of this time, though my bodily strength failed daily.
Stevens always kept me employed: at hard work as
long as I could do it, and at lighter labour, as my
strength went away. At last, finding that the Doctor's
experiments had so reduced me that I was useless in
the field, he put me to his old trade of carpentering
and joinery, which I took too very readily, and soon
got a liking for.

JOHN BROWN

2

When I caught sight of them, I turned off the main
road into the woods, hoping to escape their sight;
their horses, however, being much swifter than mine,
they soon got within a short distance of me. I then
came to a rail fence, which I found it very difficult to
get over, but breaking several rails away, I effected
my object. They then called me upon to stop more
than three times; and I not doing so, they fired after
me, but the pistol only snapped.

This is according to law; after three calls they may
shoot a runaway slave. Soon after the one on the
horse came up with me, and catching hold of the
bridle of my horse, pushed the pistol to my side; the
other soon came up, and breaking off several stout
branches from the trees, they gave me about one hundred blows. This they did very near to a planter's
house. The gentleman was not at home, but his wife
came out and begged them not to *kill me so near the
house;* they took no notice of this, but kept on beating
me. They then fastened me to the axle tree of their
chaise. One of them got into the chaise, the other took
my horse, and they ran me all the eight miles as

fast as they could; the one on my horse going behind
to guard me.

In this way we came to my old master, Mr. Gooch.
The first person I saw was himself; he unchained me
from the chaise, and at first seemed to treat me very
gently, asking me where I had been, etc. The first
thing the sons did was to show the rasp which I had
got to cut my chain. My master gave me a hearty
dinner, the best he ever did give me; but it was to
keep me from dying before he had given me all the
flogging he intended. After dinner he took me to a
log-house, stripped me quite naked, fastened a rail up
very high, tied my hands to the rail, fastened my feet
together, put a rail between my feet, and stood on
one end of it to hold me down; the two sons then
gave me fifty lashes each, the son-in-law another fifty,
and Mr. Gooch himself fifty more.

While doing this his wife came out, and begged him
not to kill me, the first act of sympathy I ever noticed
in her. When I called for water, they brought a
pail-full and threw it over my back ploughed up by
the lashes. After this, they took me to the blacksmith's
shop, got *two large bars of iron*, which they bent round
my feet, each bar *weighing twenty pounds*, and put a
heavy log-chain on my neck. This was on Saturday.
On the Monday, he chained me to the same female
slave as before. As he had to go out that day, he did
not give me the punishment which he intended to give
me every day, but at night when he came home, he
made us walk round his estate, and by all the houses
of the slaves, for them to taunt us; when we came
home he told us we must be up very early in the morning, and go to the field before the other slaves. We were
up at day-break, but we could not get on fast, on account of the heavy irons on my feet. It may be necessary to state here, that these irons were first made

red hot and bent in a circle, so as just to allow of my
feet going through; it having been cooled, and my leg
with the iron on lifted up to an anvil, it was made secure round my ankles. When I walked with these irons
on, I used to hold them up with my hands by means of
a cord. We walked *about a mile in two hours*, but
knowing the punishment he was going to inflict on us,
we made up our minds to escape into the woods, and
secret ourselves. This we did, and he not being able to
find us, which they could not do; and about twelve
o'clock, when we thought they would give up looking
for us at that time, we went on, and came to the banks
of the Catarba. Here I got a stone, and opened the
ring of the chain on her neck, and got it off; and the
chain round my neck was only passed through a ring;
as soon as I got her's off, I slipped the chain through
my ring, and got it off my own neck.* We then went
on by the banks of the river for some distance, and
found a little canoe about two feet wide. I managed
to get in, although the irons on my feet made it very
dangerous, for if I had upset the canoe, I could not
swim. The female got in after me, and gave me the
paddles, by which we got some distance down the
river. The current being very strong, it drove us
against a small island; we paddled round the island to
the other side, and then made towards the opposite
bank. Here again we were stopped by the current,
and made up to a large rock in the river, between the
island and the opposite shore. As the weather was
very rough we landed on the rock, and secured the
canoe, as it was not possible to get back to the island.
It was a very dark night and rained tremendously; and,
as the water was rising rapidly towards the top of the
rock, we gave all up for lost, and sometimes hoped,

* It may be well to state here, that the ring which fastened
the log-chain together round the female's neck, was an open
ring, similar to those used at the end of a watch chain.

and sometimes feared to hope, that we should never see the morning. But Providence was moved in our favour; the rain ceased, the water reached the edge of the rock, then receded, and we were out of danger from this cause. We remained all night upon the rock, and in the morning reached the opposite shore, and then made our way through the woods till we came to a field of Indian corn, where we plucked some of the green ears and ate them, having had nothing for two days and nights. We came to the estate of —— ——, where we met with a coloured man who knew me, and having run away himself from a bad master, he gave us some food, and told us we might sleep in the barn that night. Being very fatigued, we overslept ourselves; the proprietor came to the barn, but as I was in one corner under some Indian corn tops, and she in another, he did not perceive us, and we did not leave the barn before night, (Wednesday). We then went out, got something to eat, and strayed about the estate till Sunday. On that day, I met with some men, one of whom had irons on the same as me; he told me that his master was going out to see his friends, and that he would try and get my feet loose; for this purpose I parted with this female, fearing, that if she were caught with me, she would be forced to tell who took my irons off. The man tried some time without effect, he then gave me a file and I tried myself, but was disappointed on account of their thickness.

On the Monday I went on towards Lancaster, and got within three miles of it that night; and went towards the plantation of Mr. Crockett, as I knew some of his slaves, and hoped to get some food given me. When I got there, however, the dogs smelt me out and barked; upon which, Mr. Crockett came out, followed me with his rifle, and came up with me. He put me on a horse's back, which put me to extreme pain, from the great weight hanging at my feet. We reached Lancaster gaol that night, and he lodged me there. I was placed in the next dungeon to a man who was going to be hung. I shall never forget his cries and groans, as he prayed all night for the mercy of God. Mr. Gooch did not hear of me for several weeks; when he did, he sent his son-in-law, Mr. Anderson, after me. Mr. Gooch himself came within a mile of Lancaster, and waited until Mr. Anderson brought me. At this time I had but one of the irons on my feet, having got so thin round my ankles that I had slipped one off while in gaol. His son-in-law tied my hands, and made me walk along till we came to Mr. Gooch. As soon as we arrived at M'Daniel's Ford, two miles above the ferry, on the Catarba river, they made me wade across, themselves going on horseback. The water was very deep, and having irons on one foot and round my neck, I could not keep a footing. They dragged me along by my chain on the top of the water. It was as much as they could do to hold me by the chain, the current being very strong. They then took me home, flogged me, put extra irons on my neck and feet, and put me under the driver, with more work than ever I had before. He did not flog me so severely as before, but continued it every day. Among the instruments of torture employed, I here describe one:—This is a machine used for packing and pressing cotton. By it he hung me up by the hands, a horse, and at times, a man moving round the screw and carrying it up and down, and pressing the block into a box into which the cotton is put. At this time he hung me up for a quarter of an hour. I was carried up ten feet from the ground, when Mr. Gooch asked me if I was tired? He then let me rest for five minutes, then carried me round again, after which, he let me down and put me into the box and shut me down in it for about ten minutes. After this torture, I stayed with him several months, and did my work very well. It was about the beginning of 1832, when he took off my irons, and being in dread of him, he having threatened me with more punishment, I attempted again to escape from him. At this time I got into North Carolina: but a reward having been offered for me, a Mr. Robinson caught me, and chained me to a chair, upon which he sat up with me all night, and next day proceeded home with me. This was Saturday. Mr. Gooch had gone to church, several miles from his house. When he came back, the first thing he did was to pour some tar upon my head, then rubbed it all over my face, took a torch with pitch on, and set it on fire; he put it out before it did me very great injury, but the pain which I endured was most excruciating, nearly all my hair having been burnt off. On Monday, he puts irons on me again, weighing nearly fifty pounds. He threatened me again on the Sunday with another flogging; and on the Monday morning, before daybreak, I got away again, with my irons on, and was about three hours going a distance of two miles.* I had gone a good distance, when I met with a coloured man, who got some wedges, and took my irons off. However, I was caught again, and put into prison in Charlotte, where Mr. Gooch came, and took me back to Chester. He asked me how I got my irons off. They having been got off by a slave, I would not answer his question, for fear of getting the man punished. Upon this he put the fingers of my hands into a vice, and squeezed all my nails off. He then had my feet put on an anvil, and ordered a man to beat my toes, till he smashed some of my nails off. The marks of this treatment still remain upon me, some of my nails never having grown perfect since. He inflicted this punishment, in order to

* It must be recollected, that when a person is two miles from a house, in that part of the country, he can hide himself in the woods for weeks, and I knew a slave who was hid for six months without discovery, the trees being so thick.

get out of me how I got my irons off, but never succeeded. After this, he hardly knew what to do with
me; the whole stock of his cruelties seemed to be exhausted. He chained me down in the log-house. Soon
after this, he sent a female slave to see if I was safe.
Mr. Gooch had not secured me as he thought: but had
only run my chain through the ring, without locking it.
This I observed; and while the slave was coming, I
was employed in loosening the chain with the hand
that was not wounded. As soon as I observed her
coming, I drew the chain up tight, and she observing
that I seemed fast, went away and told her master,
who was in the field ordering the slaves. When she
was gone, I drew the chain through the ring, escaped
under the flooring of the log-house, and went on under
it, till I came out at the other side and ran on; but,
being sore and weak, I had not got a mile before I was
caught, and again carried back. He tied me up to a
tree in the woods at night, and made his slaves flog
me. I cannot say how many lashes I received; but it
was the worst flogging I ever had, and the last which
Mr. Gooch ever gave me.

MOSES ROPER

3

It has been seen that the jealousy and hatred of Mistress Epps made the daily life of her young and agile
slave completely miserable. I am happy in the belief
that on numerous occasions I was the means of
averting punishment from the inoffensive girl. In Epps'
absence the mistress often ordered me to whip her
without the remotest provocation. I would refuse,
saying that I feared my master's displeasure, and several times ventured to remonstrate with her against
the treatment Patsey received. I endeavored to impress

her with the truth that the latter was not responsible for the acts of which she complained, but that she being a slave, and subject entirely to her master's will, he alone was answerable.

At length "the green-eyed monster" crept into the soul of Epps also, and then it was that he joined with his wrathful wife in an infernal jubilee over the girl's miseries.

On a Sabbath day in hoeing time, not long ago, we were on the bayou bank, washing our clothes, as was our usual custom. Presently Patsey was missing. Epps called aloud, but there was no answer. No one had observed her leaving the yard, and it was a wonder with us whither she had gone. In the course of a couple of hours she was seen approaching from the direction of Shaw's. This man, as has been intimated, was a notorious profligate, and withal not on the most friendly terms with Epps. Harriet, his black wife, knowing Patsey's troubles, was kind to her, in consequence of which the latter was in the habit of going over to see her every opportunity. Her visits were prompted by friendship merely, but the suspicion gradually entered the brain of Epps, that another and a baser passion led her thither—that it was not Harriet she desired to meet, but rather the unblushing libertine, his neighbor. Patsey found her master in a fearful rage on her return. His violence so alarmed her that at first she attempted to evade direct answers to his questions, which only served to increase his suspicions. She finally, however, drew herself up proudly, and in a spirit of indignation boldly denied his charges.

"Missus don't give me soap to wash with, as she does the rest," said Patsey, "and you know why. I went over to Harriet's to get a piece," and saying this, she drew it forth from a pocket in her dress and exhibited it to him. "That's what I went to Shaw's for, Massa Epps," continued she; "the Lord knows that was all."

"You lie, you black wench!" shouted Epps.

"I *don't* lie, massa. If you kill me, I'll stick to that."

"Oh! I'll fetch you down. I'll learn you to go to Shaw's. I'll take the starch out of ye," he muttered fiercely through his shut teeth.

Then turning to me, he ordered four stakes to be driven into the ground, pointing with the toe of his boot to the places where he wanted them. When the stakes were driven down, he ordered her to be stripped of every article of dress. Ropes were then brought, and the naked girl was laid upon her face, her wrists and feet each tied firmly to a stake. Stepping to the piazza, he took down a heavy whip, and placing it in my hands, commanded me to lash her. Unpleasant as it was, I was compelled to obey him. Nowhere that day, on the face of the whole earth, I venture to say, was there such a demoniac exhibition witnessed as then ensued.

Mistress Epps stood on the piazza among her children, gazing on the scene with an air of heartless satisfaction. The slaves were huddled together at a little distance, their countenances indicating the sorrow of their hearts. Poor Patsey prayed piteously for mercy, but her prayers were vain. Epps ground his teeth, and stamped upon the ground, screaming at me, like a mad fiend, to strike *harder*.

"Strike harder, or *your* turn will come next, you scoundrel," he yelled.

"Oh, mercy, massa!—oh! have mercy, *do*. Oh, God! pity me," Patsey exclaimed continually, struggling fruitlessly, and the flesh quivering at every stroke.

When I had struck her as many as thirty times, I stopped, and turned round toward Epps, hoping he was satisfied; but with bitter oaths and threats, he ordered me to continue. I inflicted ten or fifteen blows more. By this time her back was covered with long welts, intersecting each other like net work. Epps was yet furious and savage as ever, demanding if she would like to go to Shaw's again, and swearing he would flog her until she wished she was in h——l. Throwing down the whip, I declared I could punish her no more. He ordered me to go on, threatening me with a severer flogging than she had received, in case of refusal. My heart revolted at the inhuman scene, and risking the consequences, I absolutely refused to raise the whip. He then seized it himself, and applied it with ten-fold greater force than I had. The painful cries and shrieks of the tortured Patsey, mingling with the loud and angry curses of Epps, loaded the air. She was terribly lacerated—I may say, without exaggeration, literally flayed. The lash was wet with blood, which flowed down her sides and dropped upon the ground. At length she ceased struggling. Her head sank listlessly on the ground. Her screams and supplications gradually decreased and died away into a low moan. She no longer writhed and shrank beneath the lash when it bit out small pieces of her flesh. I thought that she was dying!

It was the Sabbath of the Lord. The fields smiled in the warm sunlight—the birds chirped merrily amidst the foliage of the trees—peace and happiness seemed to reign everywhere, save in the bosoms of Epps and his panting victim and the silent witnesses around him. The tempestuous emotions that were raging there were little in harmony with the calm and quiet beauty of the day. I could look on Epps only with unutterable loathing and abhorrence, and thought within myself—"Thou devil, sooner or later, somewhere in the course of eternal justice, thou shalt answer for this sin!"

Finally, he ceased whipping from mere exhaustion, and ordered Phebe to bring a bucket of salt and water. After washing her thoroughly with this, I was told to take her to her cabin. Untying the ropes, I raised her in my arms. She was unable to stand, and as her head rested on my shoulder, she repeated many times, in a faint voice scarcely perceptible, "Oh, Platt —oh, Platt!" but nothing further. Her dress was replaced, but it clung to her back, and was soon stiff with blood. We laid her on some boards in the hut, where she remained a long time, with eyes closed and groaning in agony. At night Phebe applied melted tallow to her wounds, and so far as we were able, all endeavored to assist and console her. Day after day she lay in her cabin upon her face, the sores preventing her resting in any other position.

A blessed thing it would have been for her—days and weeks and months of misery it would have saved her—had she never lifted up her head in life again. Indeed, from that time forward she was not what she had been. The burden of a deep melancholy weighed heavily on her spirits. She no longer moved with that buoyant and elastic step—there was not that mirthful sparkle in her eyes that formerly distinguished her. The bounding vigor—the sprightly, laughter-loving spirit of her youth, were gone. She fell into a mournful and desponding mood, and oftentimes would start up in her sleep, and with raised hands, plead for mercy. She became more silent than she was, toiling all day in our midst, not uttering a word. A care-worn, pitiful expression settled on her face, and it was her humor now to weep, rather than rejoice. If ever there was a broken heart—one crushed and blighted by the rude grasp of suffering and misfortune—it was Patsey's.

SOLOMON NORTHUP

The Family

•··•··•··•··•··•··•··•··•··•··•··•··•··•··•··•··•··•··•

HENRY BIBB'S narrative was published in July, 1849, in a
season when several of the well-known narratives first appeared. After escaping, he returned to rescue his family
only to find, after a three-year search, that his wife, Malinda,
had been sold for adulterous purposes (1849 first edition).
The second JOSIAH HENSON extract portrays the excruciating
suffering caused by the break-up of the family unit through
slavery (1849 Boston edition).

1

The circumstances of my courtship and marriage, I
consider to be among the most remarkable events of
my life while a slave. To think that after I had determined to carry out the great idea which is so universally and practically acknowledged among all the
civilized nations of the earth, that I would be free or
die, I suffered myself to be turned aside by the fasci-
nating charms of a female, who gradually won my attention from an object so high as that of liberty;
and an object which I held paramount to all others.

But when I had arrived at the age of eighteen, which was in the year of 1833, it was my lot to be introduced to the favor of a mulatto slave girl named Malinda, who lived in Oldham County, Kentucky, about four miles from the residence of my owner. Malinda was a medium sized girl, graceful in her walk, of an extraordinary make, and active in business. Her skin was of a smooth texture, red cheeks, with dark and penetrating eyes. She moved in the highest circle* of slaves, and free people of color. She was also one of the best singers I ever heard, and was much esteemed by all who knew her, for her benevolence, talent and industry. In fact, I considered Malinda to be equalled by few, and surpassed by none, for the above qualities, all things considered.

It is truly marvellous to see how sudden a man's mind can be changed by the charms and influence of a female. The first two or three visits that I paid this dear girl, I had no intention of courting or marrying her, for I was aware that such a step would greatly obstruct my way to the land of liberty. I only visited Malinda because I liked her company, as a highly interesting girl. But in spite of myself, before I was aware of it, I was deeply in love; and what made this passion so effectual and almost irresistable, I became satisfied that it was reciprocal. There was a union of feeling, and every visit made the impression stronger and stronger. One or two other young men were paying attention to Malinda, at the same time; one of whom her mother was anxious to have her marry. This of course gave me a fair opportunity of testing Malinda's sincerity. I had just about opposition enough to

---

* The distinction among slaves is as marked, as the classes of society are in any aristocratic community. Some refusing to associate with others whom they deem beneath them in point of character, color, condition, or the superior importance of their respective masters.

make the subject interesting. That Malinda loved me above all others on earth, no one could deny. I could read it by the warm reception with which the dear girl always met me, and treated me in her mother's house. I could read it by the warm and affectionate shake of the hand, and gentle smile upon her lovely cheek. I could read it by her always giving me the preference of her company; by her pressing invitations to visit even in opposition to her mother's will. I could read it in the language of her bright and sparkling eye, penciled by the unchangeable finger of nature, that spake but could not lie. These strong temptations gradually diverted my attention from my actual condition and from liberty, though not entirely.

But oh! that I had only then been enabled to have seen as I do now, or to have read the following slave code, which is but a stereotyped law of American slavery. It would have saved me I think from having to lament that I was a husband and am the father of slaves who are still left to linger out their days in hopeless bondage. The laws of Kentucky, my native State, with Maryland and Virginia, which are said to be the mildest slave States in the Union, noted for their humanity, Christianity, and democracy, declare that "Any slave, for rambling in the night or riding horseback without leave, or running away, may be punished by whipping, cropping, and branding in the cheek, or otherwise, not rendering him unfit for labor." "Any slave convicted of petty larceny, murder, or wilfully burning of dwelling houses, may be sentenced to have his right hand cut off; to be hanged in the usual manner, or the head severed from the body, the body divided into four quarters, and head and quarters stuck up in the most public place in the county, where such act was committed."

At the time I joined my wife in holy wedlock, I was ignorant of these ungodly laws; I knew not that I was propogating victims for this kind of torture and cruelty. Malinda's mother was free, and lived in Bedford, about a quarter of a mile from her daughter; and we often met and passed off the time pleasantly. Agreeable to promise, on one Saturday evening, I called to see Malinda, at her mother's residence, with an intention of letting her know my mind upon the subject of marriage. It was a very bright moonlight night; the dear girl was standing in the door, anxiously waiting my arrival. As I approached the door she caught my hand with an affectionate smile, and bid me welcome to her mother's fireside. After having broached the subject of marriage, I informed her of the difficulties which I conceived to be in the way of our marriage; and that I could never engage myself to marry any girl only on certain conditions; near as I can recollect the substance of our conversation upon the subject, it was, that I was religiously inclined; that I intended to try to comply with the requisitions of the gospel, both theoretically and practically through life. Also that I was decided on becoming a free man before I died; and that I expected to get free by running away, and going to Canada, under the British Government. Agreement on those two cardinal questions I made my test for marriage.

I said, "I never will give my heart nor hand to any girl in marriage, until I first know her sentiments upon the all-important subjects of Religion and Liberty. No matter how well I might love her, nor how great the sacrifice in carrying out these God-given principles. And I here pledge myself from this course never to be shaken while a single pulsation of my heart shall continue to throb for Liberty." With this idea Malinda appeared to be well pleased, and with a smile she looked me in the face and said, "I have long entertained the same views, and this has been one of the greatest reasons why I have not felt inclined to enter the married state while a slave; I have always felt a desire to be free; I have long cherished a hope that I should yet be free, either by purchase or running away. In regard to the subject of Religion, I have always felt that it was a good thing, and something that I would seek for at some future period." After I found that Malinda was right upon these all important questions, and that she truly loved me well enough to make me an affectionate wife, I made proposals for marriage. She very modestly declined answering the question then, considering it to be one of a grave character, and upon which our future destiny greatly depended. And notwithstanding she confessed that I had her entire affections, she must have some time to consider the matter. To this I of course consented, and was to meet her on the next Saturday night to decide the question. But for some cause I failed to come, and the next week she sent for me, and on the Sunday evening following I called on her again; she welcomed me with all the kindness of an affectionate lover, and seated me by her side. We soon broached the old subject of marriage, and entered upon a conditional contract of matrimony, viz: that we would marry if our minds should not change within one year; that after marriage we would change our former course and live a pious life; and that we would embrace the earliest opportunity of running away to Canada for our liberty. Clasping each other by the hand, pledging our sacred honor that we would be true, we called on high heaven to witness the rectitude of our purpose. There was nothing that could be more binding upon us as slaves than this; for marriage among American slaves, is disregarded by the laws of this country. It is counted a mere temporary matter; it is a union which may be continued or broken off, with or without the consent of a slaveholder, whether he is a priest or a libertine.

There is no legal marriage among the slaves of the South; I never saw nor heard of such a thing in my life, and I have been through seven of the slave states. A slave marrying according to law, is a thing unknown in the history of American Slavery. And be it known to the disgrace of our country that every slaveholder, who is the keeper of a number of slaves of both sexes, is also the keeper of a house or houses of ill-fame. Licentious white men, can and do, enter at night or day the lodging places of slaves; break up the bonds of affection in families; destroy all their domestic and social union for life; and the laws of the country afford them no protection. Will any man count, if they can be counted, the churches of Maryland, Kentucky, and Virginia, which have slaves connected with them, living in an open state of adultery, never having been married according to the laws of the State, and yet regular members of these various denominations, but more especially the Baptist and Methodist churches? And I hazard nothing in saying, that this state of things exists to a very wide extent in the above states.

I am happy to state that many fugitive slaves, who have been enabled by the aid of an over-ruling providence to escape to the free North with those whom they claim as their wives, notwithstanding all their ignorance and superstition, are not at all disposed to live together like brutes, as they have been compelled to do in slaveholding Churches. But as soon as they get free from slavery they go before some anti-slavery clergyman, and have the solemn ceremony of marriage performed according to the laws of the country. And if they profess religion, and have been baptized by a slaveholding minister, they repudiate it after becoming free, and are rebaptized by a man who is worthy of doing it according to the gospel rule.

The time and place of my marriage, I consider one of the most trying of my life. I was opposed by friends

and foes; my mother opposed me because she thought
I was too young, and marrying she thought would in-
volve me in trouble and difficulty. My mother-in-law
opposed me, because she wanted her daughter to marry
a slave who belonged to a very rich man living nearby,
and who was well known to be the son of his master.
She thought no doubt that his master or father might
chance to set him free before he died, which would
enable him to do a better part by her daughter than I
could! And there was no prospect then of my ever
being free. But his master has neither died nor yet set
his son free, who is now about forty years of age, toiling under the lash, waiting and hoping that his master
may die and will him to be free.

The young men were opposed to our marriage for
the same reason that Paddy opposed a match when
the clergyman was about to pronounce the marriage
ceremony of a young couple. He said "if there be any
present who have any objections to this couple being
joined together in holy wedlock, let them speak now,
or hold their peace henceforth." At this time Paddy
sprang to his feet and said, "Sir, I object to this." Every
eye was fixed upon him. "What is your objection?" said
the clergyman. "Faith," replied Paddy, "Sir I want her
myself."

The man to whom I belonged was opposed, because
he feared my taking off from his farm some of the
fruits of my own labor for Malinda to eat, in the
shape of pigs, chickens, or turkeys, and would count it
not robbery. So we formed a resolution, that if we
were prevented from joining in wedlock, that we would
run away, and strike for Canada, let the consequences
be what they might. But we had one concolation;
Malinda's master was very much in favor of the match,
but entirely upon selfish principles. When I went to ask
his permission to marry Malinda, his answer was in
the affirmative with but one condition, which I con-

sider to be too vulgar to be written in this book. Our marriage took place one night during the Christmas holydays; at which time we had quite a festival given us. All appeared to be wide awake, and we had quite a jolly time at my wedding party. And notwithstanding our marriage was without license or sanction of law, we believed it to be honorable before God, and the bed undefiled. Our Christmas holydays were spent in matrimonial visiting among our friends, while it should have been spent in running away to Canada, for our liberty. But freedom was little thought of by us, for several months after marriage. I often look back to that period even now as one of the most happy seasons of my life; notwithstanding all the contaminating and heart-rending features with which the horrid system of slavery is marked, and must carry with it to its final grave, yet I still look back to that season with sweet remembrance and pleasure, that yet hath power to charm and drive back dull cares which have been accumulated by a thousand painful recollections of slavery. Malinda was to me an affectionate wife. She was with me in the darkest hours of adversity. She was with me in sorrow, and joy, in fasting and feasting, in trial and persecution, in sickness and health, in sunshine and in shade.

Some months after our marriage, the unfeeling master to whom I belonged, sold his farm with the view of moving his slaves to the State of Missouri, regardless of the separation of husbands and wives forever; but for fear of my resuming my old practice of running away, if he should have forced me to leave my wife, by my repeated requests, he was constrained to sell me to his brother, who lived within seven miles of Wm. Gatewood, who then held Malinda as his property. I was permitted to visit her only on Saturday nights, after my work was done, and I had to be at home before sunrise on Monday mornings or take a flogging. He proved to be so oppressive, and so unreasonable in punishing his victims, that I soon found I should have to run away in self-defence. But he soon began to take the hint, and sold me to Wm. Gatewood the owner of Malinda. With my new residence I confess that I was much dissatisfied. Not that Gatewood was a more cruel master than my former owner —not that I was opposed to living with Malinda, who was then the centre and object of my affections—but to live where I must be eye witness to her insults, scourgings, and abuses, such as are common to be inflicted upon slaves, was more than I could bear. If my wife must be exposed to the insults and licentious passions of wicked slavedrivers and overseers; if she must bear the stripes of the lash laid on by an unmerciful tyrant; if this is to be done with impunity, which is frequently done by slaveholders and their abettors, Heaven forbid that I should be compelled to witness the sight.

Not many months after I took up my residence on Wm. Gatewood's plantation, Malinda made me a father. The dear little daughter was called Mary Frances. She was nurtured and caressed by her mother and father, until she was large enough to creep over the floor after her parents, and climb up by a chair before I felt it to be my duty to leave my family and go into a foreign country for a season. Malinda's business was to labor out in the field the greater part of her time, and there was no one to take care of poor little Frances, while her mother was toiling in the field. She was left at the house to creep under the feet of an unmerciful old mistress, whom I have known to slap with her hand the face of little Frances, for crying after her mother, until her little face was left black and blue. I recollect that Malinda and myself came from the field one summer's day at noon, and poor little Frances came creeping to her mother smiling, but with large tear drops standing in her dear little eyes, sobbing and trying to tell her mother that she had been abused, but was not able to utter a word. Her little face was bruised black with the whole print of Mrs. Gatewood's hand. This print was plainly to be seen for eight days after it was done. But oh! this darling child was a slave; born of a slave mother. Who can imagine what could be the feelings of a father and mother, when looking upon their infant child whipped and tortured with impunity, and they placed in a situation where they could afford it no protection. But we were all claimed and held as property; the father and mother were slaves!

On this same plantation I was compelled to stand and see my wife shamefully scourged and abused by her master; and the manner in which this was done, was so violently and inhumanly committed upon the person of a female, that I despair in finding decent language to describe the bloody act of cruelty. My happiness or pleasure was then all blasted; for it was sometimes a pleasure to be with my little family even in slavery. I loved them as my wife and child. Little Frances was a pretty child; she was quiet, playful, bright, and interesting. She had a keen black eye, and the very image of her mother was stamped upon her cheek; but I could never look upon the dear child without being filled with sorrow and fearful apprehensions, of being separated by slaveholders, because she was a slave, regarded as property. And unfortunately for me, I am the father of a slave, a word too obnoxious to be spoken by a fugitive slave. It calls fresh to my mind the separation of husband and wife; of stripping, tying up and flogging; of tearing children from their parents, and selling them on the auction block. It calls to mind female virtue trampled under foot with impunity. But oh! when I remember that my daughter, my only child, is still there, destined to share the fate of all these calamities, it is too much to bear. If ever there was any one act of my life while a slave, that I have to lament over, it is that of being a father and a husband of slaves. I have the satisfaction of knowing that I am only the father of one slave. She is bone of my bone, and flesh of my flesh; poor unfortunate child. She was the first and shall be the last slave that ever I will father, for chains and slavery on this earth.

HENRY BIBB

2

The story of my life, which I am about to record, is one full of striking incident. Keener pangs, deeper joys, more singular vicissitudes, few have been led in God's providence to experience. As I look back on it through the vista of more than sixty years, and scene on scene it rises before me, an ever fresh wonder fills my mind. I delight to recall it. I dwell on it as did the Jews on the marvellous history of their rescue from the bondage of Egypt. Time has touched with its mellowing fingers its sterner features. The sufferings of the past are now like a dream, and the enduring lessons left behind make me to praise God that my soul has been tempered by him in so fiery a furnace and under such heavy blows.

I was born June 15th, 1789, in Charles County, Maryland, on a farm belonging to Mr. Francis Newman, about a mile from Port Tobacco. My mother was a slave of Dr. Josiah McPherson, but hired to the Mr. Newman to whom my father belonged. The only incident I can remember which occurred while my mother continued on Mr. Newman's farm, was the appearance one day of my father with his head bloody and his back lacerated. He was beside himself with mingled

rage and suffering. The explanation I picked up from
the conversation of others only partially explained
the matter to my mind; but as I grew older I understood it all. It seemed the overseer had sent my mother
away from the other field hands to a retired place,
and after trying persuasion in vain, had resorted to
force to accomplish a brutal purpose. Her screams
aroused my father at his distant work, and running
up, he found his wife struggling with the man. Furious
at the sight, he sprung upon him like a tiger. In a
moment the overseer was down, and, mastered by
rage, my father would have killed him but for the
entreaties of my mother, and the overseer's own promise that nothing should ever be said of the matter.
The promise was kept—like most promises of the
cowardly and debased—as long as the danger lasted.

The laws of slave states provide means and opportunities for revenge so ample, that miscreants like him
never fail to improve them. "A nigger has struck a
white man;" that is enough to set a whole county on
fire; no question is asked about the provocation. The
authorities were soon in pursuit of my father. The
fact of the sacrilegious act of lifting a hand against
the sacred temple of a white man's body—a pro-
fanity as blasphemous in the eye of a slave-state tri-
bunal as was among the Jews the entrance of a Gentile
dog into the Holy of Holies—this was all it was necessary to establish. And the penalty followed: one hundred lashes on the bare back, and to have the right
ear nailed to the whipping-post, and then severed
from the body. For a time my father kept out of the
way, hiding in the woods, and at night venturing
into some cabin in search of food. But at length the
strict watch set baffled all his efforts. His supplies cut
off, he was fairly starved out, and compelled by hunger
to come back and give himself up.

The day for the execution of the penalty was appointed. The negroes from the neighboring plantations were summoned, for their moral improvement, to witness the scene. A powerful blacksmith named Hewes laid on the stripes. Fifty were given, during which the cries of my father might be heard a mile, and then a pause ensued. True, he had struck a white man, but as valuable property he must not be damaged. Judicious men felt his pulse. Oh! he could stand the whole. Again and again the thong fell on his lacerated back. His cries grew fainter and fainter, till a feeble groan was the only response to the final blows. His head was then thrust against the post, and his right ear fastened to it with a tack; a swift pass of a knife, and the bleeding member was left sticking to the place. Then came a hurrah from the degraded crowd, and the exclamation, "That's what he's got for striking a white man." A few said, "it's a damned shame;" but the majority regarded it as but a proper tribute to their offended majesty.

It may be difficult for you, reader, to comprehend such brutality, and in the name of humanity you may protest against the truth of these statements. To you, such cruelty inflicted on a man seems fiendish. Ay, on a *man;* there hinges the whole. In the estimation of the illiterate, besotted poor whites who constituted the witnesses of such scenes in Charles County, Maryland, the man who did not feel rage enough at hearing of "a nigger" striking a white to be ready to burn him alive, was only fit to be lynched out of the neighborhood. A blow at one white man is a blow at all; is the muttering and upheaving of volcanic fires, which underlie and threaten to burst forth and utterly consume the whole social fabric. Terror is the fiercest nurse of cruelty. And when, in this our day, you find tender English women and Christian English divines fiercely urging that India should be made one pool of Sepoy blood, pause a moment before you lightly refuse to

believe in the existence of such ferocious passions in
the breasts of tyrannical and cowardly slave-drivers.

Previous to this affair my father, from all I can
learn, had been a good-humored and light-hearted
man, the ringleader in all fun at corn-huskings and
Christmas buffoonery. His banjo was the life of the
farm, and all night long at a merry-making would he
play on it while the other negroes danced. But from
this hour he became utterly changed. Sullen, morose,
and dogged, nothing could be done with him. The milk
of human kindness in his heart was turned to gall. He
brooded over his wrongs. No fear or threats of being
sold to the far south—the greatest of all terrors to the
Maryland slave—would render him tractable. So off he
was sent to Alabama. What was his after fate neither
my mother nor I have ever learned; the great day
will reveal all. This was the first chapter in my history.

After the sale of my father by Newman, Dr. McPherson would no longer hire out my mother to him. She
returned, accordingly, to his estate. He was far kinder
to his slaves than the planters generally were, never
suffering them to be struck by any one. He was a man
of good, kind impulses, liberal, jovial, hearty. No degree of arbitrary power could ever lead him to cruelty.
As the first negro-child ever born to him, I was his
especial pet. He gave me his own Christian name,
Josiah, and with that he also gave me my last name,
Henson, after an uncle of his, who was an officer in
the Revolutionary war. A bright spot in my childhood
was my residence with him—bright, but, alas! fleeting.
Events were rapidly maturing which were to change
the whole aspect of my life. The kind Doctor was not
exempt from that failing which too often besets easy,
social natures in a dissipated community. He could not
restrain his convivial propensities. Although he maintained a high reputation for goodness of heart and an

almost saint-like benevolence, the habit of intemper-
ance steadily gained ground, and finally occasioned
his death. Two negroes on the plantation found him
one morning lying dead in the middle of a narrow
stream, not a foot in depth. He had been away the
night previous at a social party, and when returning
home had fallen from his horse, probably, and being
too intoxicated to stagger through the stream, fell and
was drowned. "There's the place where massa got
drownded at"; how well I remember having it pointed
out to me in those very words.

For two or three years my mother and her young
family of six children had resided on this estate; and
we had been in the main very happy. She was a good
mother to us, a woman of deep piety, anxious above all
things to touch our hearts with a sense of religion.
How or where she acquired her knowledge of God,
or her acquaintance with the Lord's Prayer, which she
so frequently taught us to repeat, I am unable to say.
I remember seeing her often on her knees, trying to
arrange her thoughts in prayer appropriate to her situation, but which amounted to little more than constant
ejaculations, and the repetition of short phrases which
were within my infant comprehension, and have remained in my memory to this hour.

Our term of happy union as one family was now,
alas! at an end. Mournful as was the Doctor's death
to his friends it was a far greater calamity to us. The
estate and the slaves must be sold and the proceeds
divided among the heirs. We were but property—not
a mother, and the children God had given her.

Common as are slave-auctions in the southern states,
and naturally as a slave may look forward to the time
when he will be put up on the block, still the full misery
of the event—of the scenes which precede and succeed it—is never understood till the actual experience
comes. The first sad announcement that the sale is

to be; the knowledge that all ties of the past are to be sundered; the frantic terror at the idea of being sent "down south;" the almost certainty that one member of a family will be torn from another; the anxious scanning of purchasers' faces; the agony at parting, often forever, with husband, wife, child—these must be seen and felt to be fully understood. Young as I was then, the iron entered into my soul. The remembrance of the breaking up of McPherson's estate is photographed in its minutest features in my mind. The crowd collected around the stand, the huddling group of negroes, the examination of muscle, teeth, the exhibition of agility, the look of the auctioneer, the agony of my mother—I can shut my eyes and see them all.

My brothers and sisters were bid off first, and one by one, while my mother, paralyzed by grief, held me by the hand. Her turn came, and she was bought by Isaac Riley of Montgomery County. Then I was offered to the assembled purchasers. My mother, half distracted with the thought of parting forever from all her children, pushed through the crowd, while the bidding for me was going on, to the spot where Riley was standing. She fell at his feet, and clung to his knees, entreating him in tones that a mother only could command, to buy her *baby* as well as herself, and spare to her one, at least, of her little ones. Will it, can it be believed that this man, thus appealed to, was capable not merely of turning a deaf ear to her supplication, but of disengaging himself from her with such violent blows and kicks, as to reduce her to the necessity of creeping out of his reach, and mingling the groan of bodily suffering with the sob of a breaking heart? As she crawled away from the brutal man I heard her sob out, "Oh, Lord Jesus, how long, how long shall I suffer this way!" I must have been then between five and six years old. I seem to see and hear my poor weeping mother now. This was one of my earliest observations of men; an experience which I only shared with thousands of my race, the bitterness of which to any individual who suffers it cannot be diminished by the frequency of its recurrence, while it is dark enough to overshadow the whole after-life with something blacker than a funeral pall.

JOSIAH HENSON

The Women

•-•-•-•-•-•-•-•-•-•-•-•-•-•-•-•-•-•-•-•

HARRIET JACOBS is the *Pamela* of the slave narratives (1861
Boston edition). HARRIET TUBMAN, the "Moses" of her
people, needs no introduction. Sarah Hopkins Bradford compiled the 1869 edition of anecdotes for the benefit of her
friend. Harriet Tubman must surely be one of the great
women of American history. She returned indefatigably
time and again to the dangerous South to rescue some three
hundred slaves. Even in old age, she was caring for poor
children and elderly folk in her Auburn, New York, home.
ELIZABETH KECKLEY, the modiste and confidante of Mrs.
Lincoln, did much to assuage the bereavement of the President's widow. (1868 edition of *Behind the Scenes; or, Thirty
Years a Slave and Four Years in the White House, as Mrs.
Lincoln's Maid.*)

1

I would ten thousand times rather that my children
should be the half-starved paupers of Ireland than to
be the most pampered among the slaves of America.

I would rather drudge out my life on a cotton plantation, till the grave opened to give me rest, than to live
with an unprincipled master and a jealous mistress.
The felon's home in a penitentiary is preferable. He
may repent, and turn from the error of his ways, and
so find peace; but it is not so with a favorite slave.
She is not allowed to have any pride of character. It
is deemed a crime in her to wish to be virtuous.

Mrs. Flint possessed the key to her husband's character before I was born. She might have used this
knowledge to counsel and to screen the young and the
innocent among her slaves; but for them she had no
sympathy. They were the objects of her constant suspicion and malevolence. She watched her husband with
unceasing vigilance; but he was well practised in means
to evade it. What he could not find opportunity to say
in words he manifested in signs. He invented more than
were ever thought of in a deaf and dumb asylum. I
let them pass, as if I did not understand what he
meant; and many were the curses and threats bestowed
on me for my stupidity. One day he caught me teaching
myself to write. He frowned, as if he was not well
pleased; but I suppose he came to the conclusion
that such an accomplishment might help to advance
his favorite scheme. Before long, notes were often
slipped into my hand. I would return them, saying, "I
can't read them, sir." "Can't you?" he replied; "then I
must read them to you." He always finished the reading by asking, "Do you understand?" Sometimes he
would complain of the heat of the tea room, and order
his supper to be placed on a small table in the piazza.
He would seat himself there with a well-satisfied smile,
and tell me to stand by and brush away the flies. He
would eat very slowly, pausing between the mouthfuls.
These intervals were employed in describing the happiness I was so foolishly throwing away, and in threatening me with the penalty that finally awaited my

stubborn disobedience. He boasted much of the for-
bearance he had exercised towards me, and reminded
me that there was a limit to his patience. When I succeeded in avoiding opportunities for him to talk to
me at home, I was ordered to come to his office, to
do some errand. When there, I was obliged to stand
and listen to such language as he saw fit to address
to me. Sometimes I so openly expressed my contempt
for him that he would become violently enraged, and
I wondered why he did not strike me. Circumstanced
as he was, he probably thought it was better policy to
be forbearing. But the state of things grew worse and
worse daily. In desperation I told him that I must and
would apply to my grandmother for protection. He
threatened me with death, and worse than death, if I
made any complaint to her. Strange to say, I did not
despair. I was naturally of a buoyant disposition, and
always I had a hope of somehow getting out of his
clutches. Like many a poor, simple slave before me, I
trusted that some threads of joy would yet be woven
into my dark destiny.

I had entered my sixteenth year, and every day it
became more apparent that my presence was intol-
erable to Mrs. Flint. Angry words frequently passed
between her and her husband. He had never punished
me himself, and he would not allow any body else to
punish me. In that respect, she was never satisfied; but,
in her angry moods, no terms were too vile for her to
bestow upon me. Yet I, whom she detested so bitterly, had far more pity for her than he had, whose
duty it was to make her life happy. I never wronged
her, or wished to wrong her; and one word of kindness from her would have brought me to her feet.

After repeated quarrels between the doctor and his
wife, he announced his intention to take his youngest
daughter, then four years old, to sleep in his apartment. It was necessary that a servant should sleep in

the same room, to be on hand if the child stirred. I was selected for that office, and informed for what purpose that arrangement had been made. By managing to keep within sight of people, as much as possible, during the day time, I had hitherto succeeded in eluding my master, though a razor was often held to my throat to force me to change this line of policy. At night I slept by the side of my great aunt, where I felt safe. He was too prudent to come into her room. She was an old woman, and had been in the family many years. Moreover, as a married man, and a professional man, he deemed it necessary to save appearances in some degree. But he resolved to remove the obstacle in the way of his scheme; and he thought he had planned it so that he should evade suspicion. He was well aware how much I prized my refuge by the side of my old aunt, and he determined to dispossess me of it. The first night the doctor had the little child in his room alone. The next morning, I was ordered to take my station as nurse the following night. A kind Providence interposed in my favor. During the day Mrs. Flint heard of this new arrangement, and a storm followed. I rejoiced to hear it rage.

After a while my mistress sent for me to come to her room. Her first question was, "Did you know you were to sleep in the doctor's room?"

"Yes, ma'am."

"Who told you?"

"My master."

"Will you answer truly all the questions I ask?"

"Yes, ma'am."

"Tell me, then, as you hope to be forgiven, are you innocent of what I have accused you?"

"I am."

She handed me a Bible, and said, "Lay your hand on your heart, kiss this holy book, and swear before God that you tell me the truth."

I took the oath she required, and I did it with a clear conscience.

"You have taken God's holy word to testify your innocence," said she. "If you have deceived me, beware! Now take this stool, sit down, look me directly in the face, and tell me all that has passed between your master and you."

I did as she ordered. As I went on with my account her color changed frequently, she wept, and sometimes groaned. She spoke in tones so sad, that I was touched by her grief. The tears came to my eyes; but I was soon convinced that her emotions arose from anger and wounded pride. She felt that her marriage vows were desecrated, her dignity insulted; but she had no compassion for the poor victim of her husband's perfidy. She pitied herself as a martyr; but she was incapable of feeling for the condition of shame and misery in which her unfortunate, helpless slave was placed.

Yet perhaps she had some touch of feeling for me; for when the conference was ended, she spoke kindly, and promised to protect me. I should have been much comforted by this assurance if I could have had confidence in it; but my experiences in slavery had filled me with distrust. She was not a very refined woman, and had not much control over her passions. I was an object of her jealousy, and, consequently, of her hatred; and I knew I could not expect kindness or confidence from her under the circumstances in which I was placed. I could not blame her. Slaveholders' wives feel as other women would under similar circumstances. The fire of her temper kindled from small sparks, and now the flame became so intense that the doctor was obliged to give up his intended arrangement.

I knew I had ignited the torch, and I expected to suffer for it afterwards; but I felt too thankful to my mistress for the timely aid she rendered me to care much about that. She now took me to sleep in a room adjoining her own. There I was an object of her especial care, though not of her especial comfort, for she spent many a sleepless night to watch over me. Sometimes I woke up, and found her bending over me. At other times she whispered in my ear, as though it was her husband who was speaking to me, and listened to hear what I would answer. If she startled me, on such occasions, she would glide stealthily away; and the next morning she would tell me I had been talking in my sleep, and ask who I was talking to. At last, I began to be fearful for my life. It had been often threatened; and you can imagine, better than I can describe, what an unpleasant sensation it must produce to wake up in the dead of night and find a jealous woman bending over you. Terrible as this experience was, I had fears that it would give place to one more terrible.

My mistress grew weary of her vigils; they did not prove satisfactory. She changed her tactics. She now tried the trick of accusing my master of crime, in my presence, and gave my name as the author of the accusation. To my utter astonishment, he replied, "I don't believe it; but if she did acknowledge it, you tortured her into exposing me." Tortured into exposing him! Truly, Satan had no difficulty in distinguishing the color of his soul! I understood his object in making this false representation. It was to show me that I gained nothing by seeking the protection of my mistress; that the power was still all in his own hands. I pitied Mrs. Flint. She was a second wife, many years the junior of her husband; and the hoary-headed miscreant was enough to try the patience of a wiser and better woman. She was completely foiled, and knew not how to proceed. She would gladly have had me flogged for my supposed false oath; but, as I have already stated, the doctor never allowed any one to whip me. The old sinner was politic. The application of the lash might have led to remarks that would have exposed him in the eyes of his children and grandchildren. How often did I rejoice that I lived in a town where all the inhabitants knew each other! If I had been on a remote plantation, or lost among the multitude of a crowded city, I should not be a living woman at this day.

The secrets of slavery are concealed like those of the Inquisition. My master was, to my knowledge, the father of eleven slaves. But did the mothers dare to tell who was the father of their children? Did the other slaves dare to allude to it, except in whispers among themselves? No, indeed! They knew too well the terrible consequences.

My grandmother could not avoid seeing things which excited her suspicions. She was uneasy about me, and tried various ways to buy me; but the never-changing answer was always repeated: "Linda does not belong to *me*. She is my daughter's property, and I have no legal right to sell her." The conscientious man! He was too scrupulous to *sell* me; but he had no scruples whatever about committing a much greater wrong against the helpless young girl placed under his guardianship, as his daughter's property. Sometimes my persecutor would ask me whether I would like to be sold. I told him I would rather be sold to any body than to lead such a life as I did. On such occasions he would assume the air of a very injured individual, and reproach me for my ingratitude. "Did I not take you into the house, and make you the companion of my own children?" he would say. "Have I ever treated you like a negro? I have never allowed you to be punished, not even to please your mistress. And this is the recompense I get, you ungrateful girl!" I answered that he had reasons of his own for screening me from punishment, and that the course he pursued made my mistress hate me and persecute me. If I wept, he would say, "Poor child! Don't cry! don't cry! I will make peace for you with your mistress. Only let me arrange matters in my own way. Poor, foolish girl! you don't know what is for your own good. I would cherish you. I would make a lady of you. Now go, and think of all I have promised you."

I did think of it.

Reader, I draw no imaginary pictures of southern homes. I am telling you the plain truth. Yet when victims make their escape from this wild beast of Slavery, northerners consent to act the part of bloodhounds, and hunt the poor fugitive back into his den, "full of dead men's bones, and all uncleanness." Nay, more, they are not only willing, but proud, to give their daughters in marriage to slaveholders. The poor girls have romantic notions of a sunny clime, and of the flowering vines that all the year round shade a happy home. To what disappointments are they destined! The young wife soon learns that the husband in whose hands she has placed her happiness pays no regard to his marriage vows. Children of every shade of complexion play with her own fair babies, and too well she knows that they are born unto him of his own household. Jealousy and hatred enter the flowery home, and it is ravaged of its loveliness.

Southern women often marry a man knowing that he is the father of many little slaves. They do not trouble themselves about it. They regard such children as property, as marketable as the pigs on the plantation; and it is seldom that they do not make them aware of this by passing them into the slave-trader's hands as soon as possible, and thus getting them out of their sight. I am glad to say there are some honorable exceptions.

I have myself known two southern wives who exhorted their husbands to free those slaves towards whom they stood in a "parental relation"; and their request was granted. These husbands blushed before the superior nobleness of their wives' natures. Though they had only counselled them to do that which it was their duty to do, it commanded their respect, and rendered their conduct more exemplary. Concealment was at an end, and confidence took the place of distrust.

Though this bad institution deadens the moral sense, even in white women, to a fearful extent, it is not altogether extinct. I have heard southern ladies say of Mr. Such-a-one, "He not only thinks it no disgrace to be the father of those little niggers, but he is not ashamed to call himself their master. I declare, such things ought not to be tolerated in any decent society!"

HARRIET JACOBS

2

Of the very many interesting stories told me by Harriet, I cannot refrain from telling to my readers that of *Joe*, who accompanied her upon her seventh or eighth journey from Maryland to Canada.

Joe was a noble specimen of a negro, and was hired out by his master to a man for whom he worked faithfully for six years, saving him the expense of an overseer, and taking all trouble off his hands. At length this man found him so absolutely necessary to him, that he determined to buy him at any cost. His master held him proportionably high. However, by paying a thousand dollars down for him, and promising to pay another thousand in a certain time, Joe passed into the hands of his new master.

As may be imagined, Joe was somewhat surprised when the first order issued from his master's lips, was, "Now, Joe, strip and take a whipping!" Joe's experience of *whippings*, as he had seen them inflicted upon others, was not such as to cause him particularly to desire to go through the same operation on his own account; and he, naturally enough, demurred, and at first thought of resisting. But he called to mind a scene which he had witnessed a few days before, in the field, the particulars of which are too horrible and too harassing to the feelings to be given to my readers, and he thought it best to submit; but first he tried remonstrance.

"Mas'r," said he, "habn't I always been faithful to you? Habn't I worked through sun an' rain, early in de mornin', and late at night; habn't I saved you an oberseer by doin' his work; hab you anyting to complain of agin me?"

"No, Joe; I've no complaint to make of you; you're a good nigger, and you've always worked well; but the first lesson my niggers have to learn is that I am *master*, and that they are not to resist or refuse to obey anything I tell 'em to do. So the first thing they've got to do, is to be whipped; if they resist, they get it all the harder; and so I'll go on, till I kill 'em, but they've got to give up at last, and learn that I'm master."

Joe thought it best to submit. He stripped off his upper clothing, and took his whipping without a word; but as he drew his clothes up over his torn and bleeding back, he said, "Dis is de last!" That night he took a boat and went a long distance to the cabin of Harriet's father, and said, "Next time Moses comes, let me know." It was only a week or two after that, that the mysterious woman whom no one could lay their finger on appeared, and men, women, and children began to disappear from the plantations. One fine morning Joe was missing, and his brother William, from another plantation; Peter and Eliza, too, were gone; and these made part of Harriet's next party, who began their pilgrimage from Maryland to Canada, or as they expressed it, from "Egypt to de land of Canaan."

Their adventures were enough to fill a volume; they were pursued; they were hidden in "potato holes," while their pursuers passed within a few feet of them; they were passed along by friends in various disguises; they scattered and separated, to be led by guides by a roundabout way, to a meeting-place again. They were taken in by Sam Green, the man who was afterwards sent to State Prison for ten years for having a copy of "Uncle Tom's Cabin" in his house; and so, hunted and hiding and wandering, they came at last to the long bridge at the entrance of the city of Wilmington, Delaware. The rewards posted up everywhere had been at first five hundred dollars for Joe, if taken within the limits of the United States; then a thousand, and then fifteen hundred dollars, "an' all expenses clar an' clean, for his body in Easton Jail." Eight hundred for William, and four hundred for Peter, and twelve thousand for the woman who enticed them away. The long Wilmington Bridge was guarded by police officers, and the advertisements were everywhere. The party were scattered, and taken to the houses of different colored friends, and word was sent secretly to Thomas Garrett, of Wilmington, of their condition, and the necessity of their being taken across the bridge. Thomas Garrett is a Quaker, and a man of a wonderfully large and generous heart, through whose hands, Harriet tells me, two thousand self-emancipated slaves passed on their way to freedom. He was always ready, heart and hand and means, in aiding these poor fugitives, and rendered most efficient help to Harriet on many of her journeys back and forth. A letter received a few days since by the writer, from this noble-hearted philanthropist, will be given presently.

As soon as Thomas Garrett heard of the condition of these poor people, his plan was formed. He engaged two wagons, filled them with brick-layers, whom of course he paid well for their share in the enterprise, and sent them across the bridge. They went as if on a frolic, singing and shouting. The guards saw them pass, and of course expected them to re-cross the bridge. After nightfall (and fortunately it was a dark night) the same wagons went back, but with an addition to their party. The fugitives were on the bottom of the wagons, the bricklayers on the seats, still singing and shouting; and so they passed by the guards, who were entirely unsuspicious of the nature of the load the wagons contained, or of the amount of property thus escaping their hands. And so they made their way to New York. When they entered the anti-slavery office there, Joe was recognized at once by the description in the advertisement. "Well," said Mr. Oliver Johnson, "I am glad to see the man whose head is worth fifteen hundred dollars." At this Joe's heart sank. If the advertisement had got to New York, that place which it had taken them so many days and nights to reach, he thought he was in danger still. "And how far is it now to Canada?" he asked. When told how many miles, for they were to come through New York State, and cross the Suspension Bridge, he was ready to give up. "From dat time Joe was silent," said Harriet; "he sang no more, he talked no more; he sat wid his head on his hand, and nobody could 'muse him or make him take any interest in anyting." They passed along in safety, and at length found themselves in the cars, approaching Suspension Bridge. The rest were very joyous and happy, but Joe sat silent and sad. Their fellow-passengers all seemed interested in and for them, and listened with tears, as Harriet and all their party lifted up their voices and sang:

> I'm on my way to Canada,
>   That cold and dreary land;
> The sad effects of slavery,
>   I can't no longer stand.

> I've served my master all my days,
>   Widout a dime's reward;
> And now I'm forced to run away,
>   To flee the lash abroad.
> Farewell, ole master, don't think hard of me,
> I'll travel on to Canada, where all the slaves are free.
>
> The hounds are baying on my track,
>   Ole master comes behind,
> Resolved that he will bring me back,
>   Before I cross de line;
> I'm now embarked for yonder shore,
>   There a man's a man by law;
> The iron horse will bear me o'er,
>   To shake de lion's paw.
> Oh, righteous Father, wilt thou not pity me,
> And aid me on to Canada where all the slaves are free.
>
> Oh, I heard Queen Victoria say,
>   That if we would forsake
> Our native land of slavery,
>   And come across the lake;
> That she was standin' on de shore,
>   Wid arms extended wide,
> To give us all a peaceful home
>   Beyond de rolling tide.
> Farewell, ole master, etc.

The cars began to cross the bridge. Harriet was very anxious to have her companions see the Falls. William, Peter, and Eliza came eagerly to look at the wonderful sight; but Joe sat still, with his head upon his hand.

"Joe, come look at de Falls! Joe, you fool you, come see de Falls! its your last chance." But Joe sat still and never raised his head. At length Harriet knew by the rise in the center of the bridge, and the descent on the other side, that they had crossed "the line." She sprang across to Joe's seat, shook him with all her might, and shouted, "Joe, you've shook de lion's paw!" Joe did not know what she meant. "Joe, you're *free!*" shouted Harriet. Then Joe's head went up, he raised his hands on high, and his face, streaming with tears, to heaven, and broke out in loud and thrilling tones:

> Glory to God and Jesus too,
> One more soul is safe!
> Oh, go and carry de news,
> One more soul got safe.

"Joe, come and look at de Falls!" called Harriet.

> Glory to God and Jesus too,
> One more soul got safe.

was all the answer. The cars stopped on the other side. Joe's feet were the first to touch British soil, after those of the conductor.

Loud roared the waters of Niagara, but louder still ascended the anthem of praise from the overflowing heart of the freeman. And can we doubt that the strain was taken up by angel voices, and that through the arches of Heaven echoed and reechoed the strain:

> Glory to God in the Highest,
> Glory to God and Jesus too,
> One more soul is safe.

"The ladies and gentlemen gathered round him," said Harriet, "till I couldn't see Joe for the crowd, only I heard 'Glory to God and Jesus too!' louder than ever. William went after him, and pulled him, saying, 'Joe, stop your noise! you act like a fool!' Then Peter ran in and jerked him mos' off his feet,—'Joe, stop your hollerin'! Folks 'll think you're crazy!' But Joe gave no heed. The ladies were crying, and the tears like rain ran down Joe's sable cheeks. A lady reached over her fine cambric handkerchief to him. Joe wiped his face, and then he spoke."

"Oh, if I'd felt like dis down South, it would hab taken *nine* men to take me; only one more journey for me now, and dat is to Hebben!" "Well, you ole fool you," said Harriet, with whom there seems but one step from the sublime to the ridiculous, "you might a' looked at de Falls fust, and den gone to Hebben afterwards." She has seen Joe several times since, a happy and industrious freeman in Canada.

When asked, as she often is, how it was possible that she was not afraid to go back, with that tremendous price upon her head, Harriet always answers, "Why, don't I tell you, Missus, t'wan't *me*, 'twas *de Lord!* I always *tole* him, 'I trust to you. I don't know where to go or what to do, but I expect you to lead me,' an' he always did." At one time she was going down, watched for everywhere, after there had been a meeting of slaveholders in the court-house of one of the large cities of Maryland, and an added reward had been put upon her head, with various threats of the different cruel devices by which she should be tortured and put to death; friends gathered round her, imploring her not to go on directly in the face of danger and death, and this was Harriet's answer to them:

"Now look yer! John saw the city, didn't he? Yes, John saw the city. Well, what did he see? He saw twelve gates—three of dose gates was on de north—three of 'em was on de east—and three of 'em was on de west—but dere was three of 'em on de *South* too; an' I reckon if dey kill me down dere, I'll get into one of dem gates, don't you?"

Whether Harriet's ideas of the geographical bearings of the gates of the Celestial City, as seen in the Apocalyptic vision, were correct or not, we cannot doubt that she was right in the deduction her faith drew from them; and that *somewhere*, whether north, south, east, or west, to our dim vision, there is a gate to be opened for Harriet, where the welcome will be given, "Come in thou blessed of my Father."

Many of the stories told me by Harriet, in answer to questions, have been corroborated by letters, some of which will appear in this book. Of others, I have not been able to procure confirmation, owing to ignorance of the address of those conversant with the facts. I find among her papers, many of which are defaced by being carried about with her for years, portions of letters addressed to myself, by persons at the South, and speaking of the valuable assistance Harriet was rendering our soldiers in the hospital, and our armies in the field. At this time her manner of life, as related by herself, was this:

"Well, Missus, I'd go to de hospital, I would, early eb'ry mornin'. I'd get a big chunk of ice, I would, and put it in a basin, and fill it with water; den I'd take a sponge and begin. Fust man I'd come to, I'd thrash away de flies, an' dey'd rise, dey would, like bees roun' a hive. Den I'd begin to bathe der wounds, an' by de time I'd bathed off three or four, de fire and heat would have melted de ice and made de water warm, an' it would be as red as clar blood. Den I'd go an' git more ice, I would, an' by de time I got to de nex' ones, de flies would be roun' de fust ones black an' thick as eber." In this way she worked, day after day, till late at night; then she went home to her little cabin, and made about fifty pies, a great quantity of ginger-bread, and two casks of root beer. These she would hire some contraband to sell for her through the camps, and thus she would provide her support for another day; for this woman never received pay or pension, and never drew for herself but twenty days' rations during the four years of her labors. At one time she was called away from Hilton Head, by one of our officers, to come to Fernandina, where the men were "dying off like sheep," from dysentery. Harriet had acquired quite a reputation for her skill in curing this disease, by a medicine which she prepared from roots which grew near the waters which gave the disease. Here she found thousands of sick soldiers and contrabands, and immediately gave up her time and attention to them. At another time, we find her nursing those who were down by hundreds with small-pox and malignant fevers. She had never had these diseases, but she seems to have no more fear of death in one form than another. "De Lord would take keer of her till her time came, an' den she was ready to go."

When our armies and gun-boats first appeared in any part of the South, many of the poor negroes were as much afraid of "de Yankee Buckra" as of their own masters. It was almost impossible to win their confidence, or to get information from them. But to Harriet they would tell anything; and so it became quite important that she should accompany expeditions going up the rivers, or into unexplored parts of the country, to control and get information from those whom they took with them as guides.

Gen. Hunter asked her at one time if she would go with several gun-boats up the Combahee River, the object of the expedition being to take up the torpedoes placed by the rebels in the river, to destroy railroads and bridges, and to cut off supplies from the rebel troops. She said she would go if Col. Montgomery was to be appointed commander of the expedition. Col. Montgomery was one of John Brown's men, and was well known to Harriet. Accordingly, Col. Montgomery was appointed to the command, and Harriet, with several men under her, the principal of whom was J. Plowden, whose pass I have, accompanied the expedition. Harriet describes in the most graphic manner the appearance of the plantations as they passed up the river; the frightened negroes leaving their work and taking to the woods, at sight of the gun-boats; then coming to peer out like startled deer, and scudding away like the wind at the sound of the steam-whistle.

"Well," said one old negro, "Mas'r said de Yankees had horns and tails, but I nebber beliebed it till now." But the word was passed along by the mysterious telegraphic communication existing among these simple people, that these were "Lincoln's gun-boats come to set them free." In vain, then, the drivers used their whips, in their efforts to hurry the poor creatures back to their quarters; they all turned and ran for the gun-boats. They came down every road, across every field, just as they had left their work and their cabins; women with children clinging around their necks, hanging to their dresses, running behind, all making at full speed for "Lincoln's gun-boats." Eight hundred poor wretches at one time crowded the banks, with their hands extended towards their deliverers, and they were all taken off upon the gun-boats, and carried down to Beaufort.

"I nebber see such a sight," said Harriet; "we laughed, an' laughed, an' laughed. Here you'd see a woman wid a pail on her head, rice a smokin' in it just as she'd taken it from de fire, young one hangin' on behind, one han' roun' her forehead to hold on, 'tother han' diggin' into de rice-pot, eatin' wid all its might; hold of her dress two or three more; down her back a bag wid a pig in it. One woman brought two pigs, a white one, an' a black one; we took 'em all on board; named de white pig Beauregard, an' de black pig Jeff Davis. Sometimes de women would come wid twins hangin' roun' der necks; 'pears like I nebber see so many twins in my life; bags on der shoulders, baskets on der heads, and young ones taggin' behin', all loaded; pigs squealin', chickens screamin', young ones squallin'." And so they came pouring down to the gun-boats. When they stood on the shore, and the small boats put out to take them off, they all wanted to get in at once. After the boats were crowded, they would hold on to them so that they could not leave the shore. The oarsmen would beat them on their hands, but they would not let go; they were afraid the gun-boats would go off and leave them, and all wanted to make sure of one of these arks of refuge. At length Col. Montgomery shouted from the upper deck, above the clamor of appealing tones, "Moses, you'll have to give 'em a song." Then Harriet lifted up her voice and sang:

Of all the whole creation in the east or in the west,
The glorious Yankee nation is the greatest and
    the best.
Come along! Come along! don't be alarmed,
Uncle Sam is rich enough to give you all a farm.

At the end of every verse, the negroes in their enthusiasm would throw up their hands and shout "Glory," and the row-boats would take that opportunity to push off; and so at last they were all brought on board. The masters fled; houses and barns and railroad bridges were burned, tracks torn up, torpedoes destroyed, and the expedition was in all respects successful.

This fearless woman was often sent into the rebel lines as a spy, and brought back valuable information as to the position of armies and batteries; she has been in battle when the shot was falling like hail, and the bodies of dead and wounded men were dropping around her like leaves in autumn; but the thought of fear never seems to have had place for a moment in her mind. She had her duty to perform, and she expected to be taken care of till it was done.

Would that instead of taking them in this poor way at second-hand, my readers could hear this woman's graphic accounts of scenes she herself witnessed, could listen to her imitations of negro preachers in their own very peculiar dialect, her singing of camp-meeting hymns, her account of "experience meetings," her imi-

tations of the dances, and the funeral ceremonies of
these simple people. "Why, der language down dar in
de far South is jus' as different from ours in Maryland,
as you can think," said she. "Dey laughed when dey
heard me talk, an' I could not understand dem, no
how." She described a midnight funeral which she attended; for the slaves, never having been allowed to
bury their dead in the daytime, continued the custom
of night funerals from habit.

The corpse was laid upon the ground, and the people all sat round, the group being lighted up by pine
torches.

The old negro preacher began by giving out a
hymn, which was sung by all. "An' oh! I wish you
could hear 'em sing, Missus," said Harriet. "Der voices
is so sweet, and dey can sing eberyting we sing, an'
den dey can sing a great many hymns dat we can't nebber catch at all."

The old preacher began his sermon by pointing to
the dead man, who lay in a rude box on the ground
before him.

"*Shum?* Ded-a-de-dah! *Shum, David?* Ded-a-de-dah!
Now I want you all to *flec'* for moment. Who ob
all dis congregation is gwine next to lie ded-a-de-dah?
You can't go nowheres, my frien's and bredren, but
Deff 'll fin' you. You can't dig no hole so deep an' bury
yourself dar, but God A'mighty's far-seein' eye 'll fine
you, an' Deff 'll come arter you. You can't go into
that big fort (pointing to Hilton Head), an' shut yourself up dar; dat fort dat Sesh Buckner said de debil
couldn't take, but Deff'll fin' you dar. All your frien's
may forget you, but Deff 'll nebber forget you. Now,
my bredren, prepare to lie ded-a-de-dah!"

This was the burden of a very long sermon, after
which the whole congregation went round in a sort of
solemn dance, called the "spiritual shuffle," shaking
hands with each other, and calling each other by name
as they sang:

My sis'r Mary's boun' to go;
My sis'r Nanny's boun' to go;
My brudder Tony's boun' to go;
My brudder July's boun' to go.

This to the same tune, till every hand had been shaken by every one of the company. When they came to Harriet, who was a stranger, they sang:

Eberybody's boun' to go!

The body was then placed in a Government wagon, and by the light of the pine torches, the strange, dark procession moved along, singing a rude funeral hymn, till they reached the place of burial.

Harriet's account of her interview with an old negro she met at Hilton Head, is amusing and interesting. He said, "I'd been yere seventy-three years, workin' for my master widout even a dime wages. I'd worked rain-wet sun dry. I'd worked wid my mouf full of dust, but would not stop to get a drink of water. I'd been whipped, an' starved, an' I was always prayin', 'Oh! Lord, come an' delibber us!' All dat time de birds had been flyin', an' de rabens had been cryin', and de fish had been sunnin' in de waters. One day I look up, an' I see a big cloud; it didn't come up like as de clouds come out far yonder, but it 'peared to be right ober head. Der was tunders out of dat, an' der was lightnin's. Den I looked down on de water, an' I see, 'peared to me a big house in de water, an' out of de big house came great big eggs, and de good eggs went on trou' de air, an' fell into de fort; an' de bad eggs burst before dey got dar. Den de Sesh Buckra begin to run, an de neber stop running till de git to de swamp, an' de stick dar an' de die dar. Den I heard 'twas the Yankee ship* firin' out de big eggs, and dey had come to set us free. Den I praise de Lord. He come an'

* The Wabash.

put he little finger in de work, an' dey Sesh Buckra all go; and de birds stop flyin', and de rabens stop cryin', an' when I go to catch a fish to eat wid my rice, de's no fish dar. De Lord A'mighty 'd come and frightened 'em all out of de waters. Oh! Praise de Lord! I'd prayed seventy-three years, an' now he's come an' we's all free."

The last time Harriet was returning from the war, with her pass as hospital nurse, she bought a half-fare ticket, as she was told she must do; and missing the other train, she got into an emigrant train on the Amboy Railroad. When the conductor looked at her ticket, he said, "Come, hustle out of here! We don't carry niggers for half-fare." Harriet explained to him that she was in the employ of Government, and was entitled to transportation as the soldiers were. But the conductor took her forcibly by the arm, and said, "I'll make you tired of trying to stay here." She resisted, and being very strong, she could probably have got the better of the conductor, had he not called three men to his assistance. The car was filled with emigrants, and no one seemed to take her part. The only words she heard, accompanied with fearful oaths, were, "Pitch the nagur out!" They nearly wrenched her arm off, and at length threw her, with all their strength, into a baggage-car. She supposed her arm was broken, and in intense suffering she came on to New York. As she left the car, a delicate-looking young man came up to her, and, handing her a card, said, "You ought to sue that conductor, and if you want a witness, call on me." Harriet remained all winter under the care of a physician in New York; he advised her to sue the Railroad company, and said that he would willingly testify as to her injuries. But the card the young man had given her was only a visiting card, and she did not know where to find him, and so she let the matter go.

The writer here finds it necessary to apologize for the very desultory and hasty manner in which this little book is written. Being herself pressed for time, in the expectation of soon leaving the country, she is obliged to pen down the material to be used in the short and interrupted interviews she can obtain with Harriet, and also to use such letters and accounts as may be sent her, as they come, without being able to work them in, in the order of time.

In the Spring of 1860, Harriet Tubman was requested by Mr. Gerrit Smith to go to Boston to attend a large Anti-Slavery meeting. On her way, she stopped at Troy to visit a cousin, and while there, the colored people were one day startled with the intelligence that a fugitive slave, by the name of Charles Nalle, had been followed by his master (who was his younger brother, and not one grain whiter than he), and that he was already in the hands of the officers, and was to be taken back to the South. The instant Harriet heard the news, she started for the office of the U. S. Commissioner, scattering the tidings as she went. An excited crowd was gathered about the office, through which Harriet forced her way, and rushed up stairs to the door of the room where the fugitive was detained. A wagon was already waiting before the door to carry off the man, but the crowd was even then so great, and in such a state of excitement, that the officers did not dare to bring the man down. On the opposite side of the street stood the colored people, watching the window where they could see Harriet's sun-bonnet, and feeling assured that so long as she stood there, the fugitive was still in the office. Time passed on, and he did not appear. "They've taken him out another way, depend upon that," said some of the colored people. "No," replied others, "there stands 'Moses' yet, and as long as she is there, he is safe." Harriet, now seeing the necessity for a tremendous effort for his rescue, sent out some little boys to cry *fire*. The bells rang, the crowd increased, till the whole street was a dense mass of people. Again and again the officers came out to try and clear the stairs, and make a way to take their captive down; others were driven down, but Harriet stood her ground, her head bent down, and her arms folded. "Come, old woman, you must get out of this," said one of the officers; "I must have the way cleared; if you can't get down alone, someone will help you." Harriet, still putting on a greater appearance of decrepitude, twitched away from him, and kept her place. Offers were made to buy Charles from his master, who at first agreed to take twelve hundred dollars for him; but when that was subscribed, he immediately raised the price to fifteen hundred. The crowd grew more excited. A gentleman raised a window and called out, "Two hundred dollars for his rescue, but not one cent to his master!" This was responded to by a roar of satisfaction from the crowd below. At length the officers appeared, and announced to the crowd that if they would open a lane to the wagon, they would promise to bring the man down the front way.

The lane was opened, and the man was brought out —a tall, handsome, intelligent *white* man, with his wrists manacled together, walking between the U. S. Marshal and another officer, and behind him his brother and his master, so like him that one could hardly be told from the other. The moment they appeared, Harriet roused from her stooping posture, threw up a window, and cried to her friends: "Here he comes—take him!" and then darted down the stairs like a wild-cat. She seized one officer and pulled him down, then another, and tore him away from the man; and keeping her arms about the slave, she cried to her friends: "Drag us out! Drag him to the river! Drown him! but don't let them have him!" They were knocked down together, and while down she tore off her sun-bonnet and tied it on the head of the fugitive. When he rose, only his head could be seen, and amid the surging mass of people the slave was no longer recognized, while the master appeared like the slave. Again and again they were knocked down, the poor slave utterly helpless, with his manacled wrists streaming with blood. Harriet's outer clothes were torn from her, and even her stout shoes were all pulled from her feet, yet she never relinquished her hold of the man, till she had dragged him to the river, where he was tumbled into a boat, Harriet following in a ferryboat to the other side. But the telegraph was ahead of them, and as soon as they landed he was seized and hurried from her sight. After a time, some school children came hurrying along, and to her anxious inquiries they answered, "He is up in that house, in the third story." Harriet rushed up to the place. Some men were attempting to make their way up the stairs. The officers were firing down, and two men were lying on the stairs, who had been shot. Over their bodies our heroine rushed, and with the help of others burst open the door of the room, dragged out the fugitive, whom Harriet carried down stairs in her arms. A gentleman who was riding by with a fine horse, stopped to ask what the disturbance meant; and on hearing the story, his sympathies seemed to be thoroughly aroused; he sprang from his wagon, calling out, "That is a blood-horse, drive him till he drops." The poor man was hurried in; some of his friends jumped in after him, and drove at the most rapid rate to Schenectady.

HARRIET TUBMAN

3

I had never heard Mr. Lincoln make a public speech, and, knowing the man so well, was very anxious to hear him. On the morning of the Tuesday after our return from City Point, Mrs. Lincoln came to my apartments, and before she drove away I asked permission to come to the White House that night and hear Mr. Lincoln speak.

"Certainly, Lizabeth; if you take any interest in political speeches, come and listen in welcome."

"Thank you, Mrs. Lincoln. May I trespass further on your kindness by asking permission to bring a friend with me?"

"Yes, bring your friend also. By the way, come in time to dress me before the speaking commences."

"I will be in time. You may rely upon that. Good morning," I added, as she swept from my room, and, passing out into the street, entered her carriage and drove away.

About 7 o'clock that evening I entered the White House. As I went up-stairs I glanced into Mr. Lincoln's room through the half-open door, and seated by a desk was the President, looking over his notes and muttering to himself. His face was thoughtful, his manner abstracted, and I knew, as I paused a moment to watch him, that he was rehearsing the part that he was to play in the great drama soon to commence.

Proceeding to Mrs. Lincoln's apartment, I worked with busy fingers, and in a short time her toilette was completed.

Great crowds began to gather in front of the White House, and loud calls were made for the President. The band stopped playing, and as he advanced to the centre window over the door to make his address, I looked out, and never saw such a mass of heads before. It was like a black, gently swelling sea. The swaying motion of the crowd, in the dim, uncertain light, was like the rising and falling of billows—like the ebb and flow of the tide upon the stranded shore of the ocean. Close to the house the faces were plainly discernible, but they faded into mere ghostly outlines on the outskirts of the assembly; and what added to the weird, spectral beauty of the scene, was the confused hum of voices that rose above the sea of forms, sounding like the subdued, sullen roar of an ocean storm, or the wind soughing through the dark lonely forest. It was a grand and imposing scene, and when the President, with pale face and his soul flashing through his eyes, advanced to speak, he looked more like a demigod than a man crowned with the fleeting days of mortality.

The moment the President appeared at the window he was greeted with a storm of applause, and voices re-echoed the cry, "A light! a light!"

A lamp was brought, and little Tad at once rushed to his father's side, exclaiming:

"Let me hold the light, Papa! let me hold the light!"

Mrs. Lincoln directed that the wish of her son be gratified, and the lamp was transferred to his hands. The father and son standing there in the presence of thousands of free citizens, the one lost in a chain of eloquent ideas, the other looking up into the speaking face with a proud, manly look, formed a beautiful and striking tableau.

There were a number of distinguished gentlemen, as well as ladies, in the room, nearly all of whom remarked the picture.

I stood a short distance from Mr. Lincoln, and as the light from the lamp fell full upon him, making him stand out boldly in the darkness, a sudden thought struck me, and I whispered to the friend at my side:

"What an easy matter would it be to kill the President, as he stands there! He could be shot down from the crowd, and no one be able to tell who fired the shot."

I do not know what put such an idea into my head, unless it was the sudden remembrance of the many warnings that Mr. Lincoln had received.

The next day, I made mention to Mrs. Lincoln of

the idea that had impressed me so strangely the night before, and she replied with a sigh:

"Yes, yes, Mr. Lincoln's life is always exposed. Ah, no one knows what it is to live in constant dread of some fearful tragedy. The President has been warned so often, that I tremble for him on every public occasion. I have a presentiment that he will meet with a sudden and violent end. I pray God to protect my beloved husband from the hands of the assassin."

Mr. Lincoln was fond of pets. He had two goats that knew the sound of his voice, and when he called them they would come bounding to his side. In the warm bright days, he and Tad would sometimes play in the yard with these goats, for an hour at a time. One Saturday afternoon I went to the White House to dress Mrs. Lincoln. I had nearly completed my task when the President came in. It was a bright day, and walking to the window, he looked down into the yard, smiled, and, turning to me, asked:

"Madam Elizabeth, you are fond of pets, are you not?"

"O yes, sir," I answered.

"Well, come here and look at my two goats. I believe they are the kindest and best goats in the world. See how they sniff the clear air, and skip and play in the sunshine. Whew! what a jump," he exclaimed as one of the goats made a lofty spring. "Madam Elizabeth, did you ever before see such an active goat?" Musing a moment, he continued: "He feeds on my bounty, and jumps with joy. Do you think we could call him a bounty-jumper? But I flatter the bounty-jumper. My goat is far above him. I would rather wear his horns and hairy coat through ilfe, than demean myself to the level of the man who plunders the national treasury in the name of patriotism. The man who enlists into the service for a consideration, and deserts the moment he receives his money but to repeat the play, is bad enough; but the men who manipulate the grand machine and who simply make the bounty-jumper their agent in an outrageous fraud are far worse. They are beneath the worms that crawl in the dark hidden places of earth."

His lips curled with haughty scorn, and a cloud was gathering on his brow. Only a moment the shadow rested on his face. Just then both goats looked up at the window and shook their heads as if they would say "How d'ye do, old friend?"

"See, Madam Elizabeth," exclaimed the President in a tone of enthusiasm, "my pets recognize me. How earnestly they look! There they go again; what jolly fun!" and he laughed outright as the goats bounded swiftly to the other side of the yard. Just then Mrs. Lincoln called out, "Come, Lizabeth; if I get ready to go down this evening I must finish dressing myself, or you must stop staring at those silly goats."

Mrs. Lincoln was not fond of pets, and she could not understand how Mr. Lincoln could take so much delight in his goats. After Willie's death, she could not bear the sight of anything he loved, not even a flower. Costly bouquets were presented to her, but she turned from them with a shudder, and either placed them in a room where she could not see them, or threw them out of the window. She gave all of Willie's toys—everything connected with him—away, as she said she could not look upon them without thinking of her poor dead boy, and to think of him, in his white shroud and cold grave, was maddening. I never in my life saw a more peculiarly constituted woman. Search the world over, and you will not find her counterpart. After Mr. Lincoln's death, the goats that he loved so well were given away—I believe to Mrs. Lee, née Miss Blair, one of the few ladies with whom Mrs. Lincoln was on intimate terms in Washington.

During my residence in the Capital I made my home

with Mr. and Mrs. Walker Lewis, people of my own race, and friends in the truest sense of the word.

The days passed without any incident of particular note disturbing the current of life. On Friday morning, April 14th—alas! what American does not remember the day—I saw Mrs. Lincoln but for a moment. She told me that she was to attend the theatre that night with the President, but I was not summoned to assist her in making her toilette. Sherman had swept from the northern border of Georgia through the heart of the Confederacy down to the sea, striking the death-blow to the rebellion. Grant had pursued General Lee beyond Richmond, and the army of Virginia, that had made such stubborn resistance, was crumbling to pieces. Fort Sumter had fallen;—the stronghold first wrenched from the Union, and which had braved the fury of Federal guns for so many years, was restored to the Union; the end of the war was near at hand, and the great pulse of the loyal North thrilled with joy. The dark war-cloud was fading, and a white-robed angel seemed to hover in the sky, whispering "Peace—peace on earth, good-will toward men!" Sons, brothers, fathers, friends, sweethearts were coming home. Soon the white tents would be folded, the volunteer army be disbanded, and tranquility again reign. Happy, happy day!—happy at least to those who fought under the banner of the Union. There was great rejoicing throughout the North. From the Atlantic to the Pacific, flags were gaily thrown to the breeze, and at night every city blazed with its tens of thousand lights. But scarcely had the fireworks ceased to play, and the lights been taken down from the windows, when the lightning flashed the most appalling news over the magnetic wires. "The President has been murdered!" spoke the swift-winged messenger, and the loud huzza died upon the lips. A nation suddenly paused in the midst of festivity, and stood paralyzed with horror—transfixed with awe.

Oh, memorable day! Oh, memorable night! Never before was joy so violently contrasted with sorrow.

At 11 o'clock at night I was awakened by an old friend and neighbor, Miss M. Brown, with the startling intelligence that the entire Cabinet had been assassinated, and Mr. Lincoln shot, but not mortally wounded. When I heard the words I felt as if the blood had been frozen in my veins, and that my lungs must collapse for the want of air. Mr. Lincoln shot! the Cabinet assassinated! What could it mean? The streets were alive with wondering, awe-stricken people. Rumors flew thick and fast, and the wildest reports came with every new arrival. The words were repeated with blanched cheeks and quivering lips. I waked Mr. and Mrs. Lewis, and told them that the President was shot, and that I must go to the White House. I could not remain in a state of uncertainty. I felt that the house would not hold me. They tried to quiet me, but gentle words could not calm the wild tempest. They quickly dressed themselves, and we sallied out into the street to drift with the excited throng. We walked rapidly towards the White House, and on our way passed the residence of Secretary Seward, which was surrounded by armed soldiers, keeping back all intruders with the point of the bayonet. We hurried on, and as we approached the White House, saw that it too was surrounded with soldiers. Every entrance was strongly guarded, and no one was permitted to pass. The guard at the gate told us that Mr. Lincoln had not been brought home, but refused to give any other information. More excited than ever, we wandered down the street. Grief and anxiety were making me weak, and as we joined the outskirts of a large crowd, I began to feel as meek and humble as a penitent child. A gray-haired old man was passing. I caught a glimpse of his face, and it seemed so full of kindness and sorrow that I gently touched his arm, and imploringly asked:

"Will you please, sir, to tell me whether Mr. Lincoln is dead or not?"

"Not dead," he replied, "but dying. God help us!" and with a heavy step he passed on.

"Not dead, but dying! then indeed God help us!" We learned that the President was mortally wounded—that he had been shot down in his box at the theatre, and that he was not expected to live till morning; when we returned home with heavy hearts. I could not sleep. I wanted to go to Mrs. Lincoln, as I pictured her wild with grief; but then I did not know where to find her, and I must wait till morning. Never did the hours drag so slowly. Every moment seemed an age, and I could do nothing but walk about and hold my arms in mental agony.

Morning came at last, and a sad morning was it. The flags that floated so gaily yesterday now were draped in black, and hung in silent folds at half-mast. The President was dead, and a nation was mourning for him. Every house was draped in black, and every face wore a solemn look. People spoke in subdued tones, and glided whisperingly, wonderingly, silently about the streets.

About eleven o'clock on Saturday morning a carriage drove up to the door, and a messenger asked for "Elizabeth Keckley."

"Who wants her?" I asked.

"I come from Mrs. Lincoln. If you are Mrs. Keckley, come with me immediately to the White House."

I hastily put on my shawl and bonnet, and was driven at a rapid rate to the White House. Everything about the building was sad and solemn. I was quickly shown to Mrs. Lincoln's room, and on entering, saw Mrs. L. tossing uneasily about upon a bed. The room was darkened, and the only person in it besides the widow of the President was Mrs. Secretary Welles, who had spent the night with her. Bowing to Mrs. Welles, I went to the bedside.

"Why did you not come to me last night, Elizabeth —I sent for you?" Mrs. Lincoln asked in a low whisper.

"I did try to come to you, but I could not find you," I answered, as I laid my hand upon her hot brow.

I afterwards learned, that when she had partially recovered from the first shock of the terrible tragedy in the theatre, Mrs. Welles asked:

"Is there no one, Mrs. Lincoln, that you desire to have with you in this terrible affliction?"

"Yes, send for Elizabeth Keckley. I want her just as soon as she can be brought here."

Three messengers, it appears, were successively despatched for me, but all of them mistook the number and failed to find me.

Shortly after entering the room on Saturday morning, Mrs. Welles excused herself, as she said she must go to her own family, and I was left alone with Mrs. Lincoln.

She was nearly exhausted with grief, and when she became a little quiet, I asked and received permission to go into the Guests' Room, where the body of the President lay in state. When I crossed the threshold of the room, I could not help recalling the day on which I had seen little Willie lying in his coffin where the body of his father now lay. I remembered how the President had wept over the pale beautiful face of his gifted boy, and now the President himself was dead. The last time I saw him he spoke kindly to me, but alas! the lips would never move again. The light had faded from his eyes, and when the light went out the soul went with it. What a noble soul was his—noble in all the noble attributes of God! Never did I enter the solemn chamber of death with such palpitating heart and trembling footsteps as I entered it that day. No common mortal had died. The Moses of my people had fallen in the hour of his triumph. Fame had woven her choicest chaplet for his brow. Though the brow was cold and pale in death, the chaplet should not fade, for God had studded it with the glory of the eternal stars.

When I entered the room, the members of the Cabinet and many distinguished officers of the army were grouped around the body of their fallen chief. They made room for me, and, approaching the body, I lifted the white cloth from the white face of the man that I had worshipped as an idol—looked upon as a demigod. Notwithstanding the violence of the death of the President, there was something beautiful as well as grandly solemn in the expression of the placid face. There lurked the sweetness and gentleness of childhood, and the stately grandeur of god-like intellect. I gazed long at the face, and turned away with tears in my eyes and a choking sensation in my throat. Ah! never was man so widely mourned before. The whole world bowed their heads in grief when Abraham Lincoln died.

Returning to Mrs. Lincoln's room, I found her in a new paroxysm of grief. Robert was bending over his mother with tender affection, and little Tad was crouched at the foot of the bed with a world of agony in his young face. I shall never forget the scene —the wails of a broken heart, the unearthly shrieks, the terrible convulsions, the wild, tempestuous outbursts of grief from the soul. I bathed Mrs. Lincoln's head with cold water, and soothed the terrible tornado as best I could. Tad's grief at his father's death was as great as the grief of his mother, but her terrible outbursts awed the boy into silence. Sometimes he would throw his arms around her neck, and exclaim, between his broken sobs, "Don't cry so, Mamma! don't cry, or you will make me cry, too! You will break my heart."

Mrs. Lincoln could not bear to hear Tad cry, and

when he would plead to her not to break his heart, she would calm herself with a great effort, and clasp her child in her arms.

Every room in the White House was darkened, and everyone spoke in subdued tones, and moved about with muffled tread. The very atmosphere breathed of the great sorrow which weighed heavily upon each heart. Mrs. Lincoln never left her room, and while the body of her husband was being borne in solemn state from the Atlantic to the broad prairies of the West, she was weeping with her fatherless children in her private chamber. She denied admittance to almost every one, and I was her only companion, except her children, in the days of her great sorrow.

There were many surmises as to who was implicated with J. Wilkes Booth in the assassination of the President. A new messenger had accompanied Mr. and Mrs. Lincoln to the theatre on that terrible Friday night. It was the duty of this messenger to stand at the door of the box during the performance, and thus guard the inmates from all intrusion. It appears that the messenger was carried away by the play, and so neglected his duty that Booth gained easy admission to the box. Mrs. Lincoln firmly believed that this messenger was implicated in the assassination plot.

One night I was lying on a lounge near the bed occupied by Mrs. Lincoln. One of the servants entering the room, Mrs. L. asked:

"Who is on watch to-night?"

"The new messenger," was the reply.

"What! the man who attended us to the theatre on the night my dear, good husband was murdered! He, I believe, is one of the murderers. Tell him to come in to me."

The messenger had overheard Mrs. Lincoln's words through the half-open door, and when he came in he was trembling violently.

She turned to him fiercely: "So you are on guard to-night—on guard in the White House after helping to murder the President!"

"Pardon me, but I did not help to murder the President. I could never stoop to murder—much less to the murder of so good and great a man as the President."

"But it appears that you *did* stoop to murder."

"No, no! don't say that," he broke in. "God knows that I am innocent."

"I don't believe you. Why were you not at the door to keep the assassin out when he rushed into the box?"

"I did wrong, I admit, and I have bitterly repented it, but I did not help to kill the President. I did not believe that any one would try to kill so good a man in such a public place, and the belief made me careless. I was attracted by the play, and did not see the assassin enter the box."

"But you should have seen him. You had no business to be careless. I shall always believe that you are guilty. Hush! I shan't hear another word," she exclaimed, as the messenger essayed to reply. "Go now and keep your watch," she added, with an imperious wave of her hand. With mechanical step and white face the messenger left the room, and Mrs. Lincoln fell back on her pillow, covered her face with her hands, and commenced sobbing.

Robert was very tender to his mother in the days of her sorrow.

He suffered deeply, as his haggard face indicated, but he was ever manly and collected when in the presence of his mother. Mrs. Lincoln was extremely nervous, and she refused to have anybody about her but myself. Many ladies called, but she received none of them. Had she been less secluded in her grief, perhaps she would have had many warmer friends to-day than she has. But far be it from me to harshly judge the sorrow of any one. Could the ladies who called to condole with Mrs. Lincoln, after the death of her husband, and who were denied admittance to her chamber, have seen how completely prostrated she was with grief, they would have learned to speak more kindly of her. Often at night, when Tad would hear her sobbing, he would get up, and come to her bed in his white sleeping-clothes: "Don't cry, Mamma; I cannot sleep if you cry! Papa was good, and he has gone to heaven. He is happy there. He is with God and brother Willie. Don't cry, Mamma, or I will cry too."

The closing appeal always proved the most effectual, as Mrs. Lincoln could not bear to hear her child cry.

Tad had been petted by his father, but petting could not spoil such a manly nature as his. He seemed to realize that he was the son of a President—to realize it in its loftiest and noblest sense. One morning, while being dressed, he looked up at his nurse, and said: "Pa is dead. I can hardly believe that I shall never see him again. I must learn to take care of myself now." He looked thoughtful a moment, then added, "Yes, Pa is dead, and I am only Tad Lincoln now, little Tad, like other little boys. I am not a President's son now. I won't have many presents any more. Well, I will try and be a good boy, and will hope to go some day to Pa and brother Willie, in heaven." He was a brave, manly child, and knew that influence had passed out of their hands with the death of his father, and that his position in life was altered. He seemed to feel that people petted him, and gave him presents, because they wanted to please the President of the United States. From that period forward he became more independent, and in a short time learned to dispense with the services of a nurse. While in Chicago, I saw him get out his clothes one Sunday morning and dress himself, and the change was such a great one to me—for while in the White House, servants obeyed his every nod and bid—that I could scarcely refrain from shedding tears. Had his father lived, I knew it would have been different with his favorite boy. Tad roomed with Robert, and he always took pride in pleasing his brother.

After the Committee had started West with the body of the President, there was quite a breeze of excitement for a few days as to where the remains should be interred. Secretary Stanton and others held frequent conferences with Robert, Mr. Todd, Mrs. Lincoln's cousin, and Dr. Henry, an old schoolmate and friend of Mr. Lincoln. The city authorities of Springfield had purchased a beautiful plot of ground in a prosperous portion of the city, and work was rapidly progressing on the tomb, when Mrs. Lincoln made strenuous objection to the location. She declared that she would stop the body in Chicago before it should be laid to rest in the lot purchased for the purpose by the City of Springfield. She gave as a reason, that it was her desire to be laid by the side of her husband when she died, and that such would be out of the question in a public place of the kind. As is well known, the difficulty was finally settled by placing the remains of the President in the family vault at Oak Ridge, a charming spot for the home of the dead.

After the President's funeral Mrs. Lincoln rallied, and began to make preparations to leave the White House. One day she suddenly exclaimed: "God, Elizabeth, what a change! Did ever woman have to suffer so much and experience so great a change? I had an ambition to be Mrs. President; that ambition has been gratified, and now I must step down from the pedestal. My poor husband! had he never been President, he might be living to-day. Alas! all is over with me!"

Folding her arms for a few moments, she rocked back and forth, then commenced again, more vehemently than ever: "My God, Elizabeth, I can never go back to Springfield! no, never, until I go in my shroud to be laid by my dear husband's side, and may Heaven speed that day! I should like to live for my sons, but life is so full of misery that I would rather die." And then she would go off into a fit of hysterics.

ELIZABETH KECKLEY

Superstition

The second extract from HENRY BIBB (1849 edition) illustrates how the fear induced by slavery led to superstition. The second extract from WILLIAM GRIMES (1825 edition) shows how the old colored woman, Frankee, was a real witch for him.

1

There is much superstition among the slaves. Many of them believe in what they call "conjuration," tricking, and witchcraft; and some of them pretend to understand the art, and say that by it they can prevent their masters from exercising their will over their slaves. Such are often applied to by others, to give them power to prevent their masters from flogging them. The remedy is most generally some kind of bitter root; they are directed to chew it and spit towards their masters when they are angry with their slaves. At other times they prepare certain kinds of powders, to sprinkle about their masters dwellings. This is all done for the purpose of defending themselves in some peaceable manner, although I am satisfied that there is no virtue at all in it. I tried it to perfection when I was a slave at the South. I was then a young man, full of life and vigor, and was very fond of visiting our neighbors' slaves, but had no time to visit only Sundays, when I could get a permit to go, or after night, when I could slip off without being seen. If it was found out, the next morning I was called up to give an account of myself for going off without permission; and would very often get a flogging for it.

I got myself into a scrape at a certain time, by going off in this way, and I expected to be severely punished for it. I had a strong notion of running off, to escape being flogged, but was advised by a friend to go to one of those conjurers, who could prevent me from being flogged. I went and informed him of the difficulty. He said if I would pay him a small sum, he would prevent my being flogged. After I had paid him, he mixed up some alum, salt and other stuff into a powder, and said I must sprinkle it about my master, if he should offer to strike me; this would prevent him. He also gave me some kind of bitter root to chew, and spit towards him, which would certainly prevent my being flogged. According to order I used his remedy, and for some cause I was let pass without being flogged that time.

I had then great faith in conjuration and witchcraft. I was led to believe that I could do almost as I pleased, without being flogged. So on the next Sabbath my conjuration was fully tested by my going off, and staying away until Monday morning, without permission. When I returned home, my master declared that he would punish me for going off; but I did not believe that he could do it, while I had this root and dust; and as he approached me, I commenced talking saucy to him. But he soon convinced me that there was no virtue in them. He became so enraged at me for saucing him, that he grasped a handful of switches and punished me severely, in spite of all my roots and powders.

But there was another old slave in that neighborhood, who professed to understand all about conjuration, and I thought I would try his skill. He told me that the first one was only a quack, and if I would only pay him a certain amount in cash, that he would tell me how to prevent any person from striking me. After I had paid him his charge, he told me to go to the cowpen after night, and get some fresh cow manure, and mix it with red pepper and white people's hair, all to be put into a pot over the fire, and scorched until it could be ground into snuff. I was then to sprinkle it about my master's bedroom, in his hat and boots, and it would prevent him from ever abusing me in any way. After I got it already prepared, the smallest pinch of it scattered over a room was enough to make a horse sneeze from the strength of it; but it did no good. I tried it to my satisfaction. It was my business to make fires in my master's chamber, night and morning. Whenever I could get a chance, I sprinkled a little of this dust about the linen of the bed, where they would breathe it on retiring. This was to act upon them as what is called a kind of love powder, to change their sentiments of anger, to those of love, towards me, but this all proved to be vain imagination. The old man had my money, and I was treated no better for it.

One night when I went in to make a fire, I availed myself of the opportunity of sprinkling a very heavy charge of this powder about my master's bed. Soon after their going to bed, they began to cough and sneeze. Being close around the house, watching and listening, to know what the effect would be, I heard them ask each other what in the world it could be, that made them cough and sneeze so. All the while, I was trembling with fear, expecting every moment I should be called and asked if I knew any thing about it. After this, for fear they might find me out in my dangerous experiments upon them, I had to give them up, for the time being. I was then convinced that running away was the most effectual way by which a slave could escape cruel punishment.

As all the instrumentalities, which I as a slave could bring to bear upon the system, had utterly failed to palliate my sufferings, all hope and consolation fled. I must be a slave for life, and suffer under the lash or die. The influence which this had only tended to make me more unhappy. I resolved that I would be free if running away could make me so. I had heard that Canada was a land of liberty, somewhere in the North; and every wave of trouble that rolled across my breast, caused me to think more and more about Canada, and liberty. But more especially after having been flogged, I have fled to the highest hills of the forest, pressing my way to the North for refuge; but the river Ohio was my limit. To me it was an impassable gulf. I had no rod wherewith to smite the stream, and thereby divide the waters. I had no Moses to go before me and lead the way from bondage to a promised land. Yet I was in a far worse state than Egyptian bondage; for they had houses and land; I had none; they had oxen and sheep; I had none; they had a wise counsel, to tell them what to do, and where to go, and even to go with them; I had none. I was surrounded by opposition on every hand. My friends were few and far between. I have often felt when running away as if I had scarcely a friend on earth.

Sometimes standing on the Ohio River bluff, looking over on a free State, and as far north as my eyes could see, I have eagerly gazed upon the blue sky of the free North, which at times constrained me to cry out from the depths of my soul, Oh! Canada, sweet land of rest—Oh! when shall I get there? Oh, that I had the wings of a dove, that I might soar away to where there is no slavery; no clanking of chains, no captives, no lacerating of backs, no parting of husbands and wives; and where man ceases to be the property of his fellow man. These thoughts have revolved in my mind a thousand times. I have stood upon the lofty banks of the river Ohio, gazing upon the splendid steamboats, wafted with all their magnificence up and down the river, and I thought of the fishes of the water, the fowls of the air, the wild beasts of the forest, all appeared to be free, to go just where they pleased, and I was an unhappy slave!

But my attention was gradually turned in a measure from this subject, by being introduced into the society of young women. This for the time being took my attention from running away, as waiting on the girls appeared to be perfectly congenial to my nature. I wanted to be well thought of by them, and would go to great lengths to gain their affection. I had been taught by the old superstitious slaves, to believe in conjuration, and it was hard for me to give up the notion, for all I had been deceived by them. One of these conjurers, for a small sum agreed to teach me to make any girl love me that I wished. After I had paid him, he told me to get a bull frog, and take a certain bone out of the frog, dry it, and when I got a chance I must step up to any girl whom I wished to make love me, and scratch her somewhere on her naked skin with this bone, and she would be certain to love me, and would follow me in spite of herself; no matter who she might be engaged to, nor who she might be walking with.

So I got me a bone for a certain girl, whom I knew to be under the influence of another young man. I happened to meet her in the company of her lover, one Sunday evening, walking out; so when I got a chance I fetched her a tremendous rasp across her neck with this bone, which made her jump. But in place of making her love me, it only made her angry with me. She felt more like running after me to retaliate on me for thus abusing her, than she felt like loving me. After I found there was no virtue in the bone of a frog, I thought I would try some other way to carry out my object. I then sought another counsellor among the old superstitious influential slaves; one who professed to be a great friend of mine, told me to get a lock of hair from the head of any girl, and wear it in my shoes: this would cause her to love me above all other persons. As there was another girl whose affections I was anxious to gain, but could not succeed, I thought, without trying the experiment of this hair. I slipped off one night to see the girl, and asked her for a lock of her hair; but she refused to give it. Believing that my success depended greatly upon this bunch of hair, I was bent on having a lock before I left that night let it cost what it might. As it was time for me to start home in order to get any sleep that night, I grasped hold of a lock of her hair, which caused her to screech, but I never let go until I had pulled it out. This of course made the girl mad with me, and I accomplished nothing but gained her displeasure.

Such are the superstitious notions of the great masses of southern slaves. It is given to them by tradition, and can never be erased, while the doors of education are bolted and barred against them.

HENRY BIBB

2

I will state to my readers some facts relative to the treatment I received from him [Colonel Thornton], and others, during the time I lived there. He had an old black female slave whom he called Frankee. I al-

ways believed her to be a witch: circumstances to
prove this, I shall hereafter state. He also had at one
time, a number of carpenters at work in his yard. One
of them, a man about my size, and resembling me very
much in his dress, being dressed in a blue roundabout
jacket. He came into the yard to his work one morning,
with an umbrella in his hand. This old woman saw
him come in, and thinking it was me, or pretending
so to do, was the cause of my receiving a severe
whipping, in the following manner. My master having
mislaid his umbrella, had been looking for it for some
time, and on enquiring of her about it, she told him
that she saw me come into the yard with it in my
hand. I was then in the yard; he called to me, and
said, where have you been sir? I replied, only to work
about the yard sir. He then asked me where I was all
night with his umbrella. I told him I had not been out
of the yard, nor had I seen his umbrella. He said I was
a liar, and that I had taken his umbrella away, and
was seen to return with it in my hand this morning
when coming into the yard. I told him it was not so,
and that I knew nothing about it. He immediately
fell foul of me with a large stick, and beat me most
unmercifully, until I really thought he would kill me.
I begged of him to desist, as I was perfectly innocent.
He, not believing me, still continued to beat me, until
his strength was entirely exhausted. Some time after
this, my mistress found his umbrella where she had
placed it herself, having removed it from the place
where he had left it, and gave it to him, saying, you
have beat him for nothing, he was innocent of it. I
was afterwards informed by another servant, of the
circumstance. I then went to my master, and told
him that he had beaten me most unmercifully, for a
crime I was not guilty of, all through the insinuation
of that old woman. He replied, "no, by Gad, I never
hit you a blow amiss; if you did not deserve it now, you

did some other time." I told him she must have been drunk or she would not have told him such a story. He said that could not be, as she never was allowed to have any liquor by her. I told him to look in her chest, and convince himself. He then enquired of her if she had any rum. She said, no, sir, I have not a drop. I then told him that if he would look in her chest, he would find it. He accordingly went, and found it. He then said to her, hey, you old bitch I have caught you in a lie. On this same account she appeared to be determined to kill me, by some means or other. I slept in the same room with her under the kitchen. My blankets were on the floor. She had a straw bed on a bed-stead about four paces from mine. My master slept directly over my head. I have heretofore stated that I was convinced that this creature was a witch, and would turn herself into almost any different shape she chose. I have at different times of the night felt a singular sensation, such as people generally call the night-mare: I would feel her coming towards me, and endeavouring to make a noise, which I could quite plainly at first; but the nearer she approached me the more faintly I would cry out. I called to her, aunt Frankee, aunt Frankee, as plain as I could, until she got upon me and began to exercise her enchantments on me. I was then entirely speechless; making a noise like one apparently choking, or strangling. My master had often heard me make this noise in the night, and had called to me, to know what was the matter; but as long as she remained there I could not answer. She would then leave me and go to her own bed. After my master had called to her a number of times, Frankee, Frankee, when she got to her own bed, she would answer, sair. What ails Theo? (a name I went by there, cutting short the name Theodore). She answered, hag ride him sair. He then called to me, telling me to go and sleep with her. I could then, after she had left me, speak myself, and also have use of my limbs. I got up, and went to her bed, and tried to get under her coverlid; but could not find her. I found her bed clothes wet. I kept feeling for her, but could not find her. Her bed was tumbled from head to foot. I was then convinced she was a witch, and that she rode me. I then lay across the corner of her bed without any covering, because I thought she would not dare to ride me on her own bed, although she was a witch. I have often, at the time she started from her own bed, in some shape or other, felt a shock, and the nigher she advanced towards me, the more severe the shock would be. The next morning my master asked me what was the matter of me last night. I told him that some old witch rode me, and that old witch, is no other than old Frankee. He cursed me and called me a damned fool, and told me that if he heard any more of it, he would whip me. I then knew he did not believe in witch-craft. He said, why don't she ride me? I will give her a dollar. Ride me, you old hag, and I will give you a dollar. I told him she would not dare to ride him.

WILLIAM GRIMES

Adventure

●··●··●··●··●··●··●··●··●··●··●··●··●··●··●··●··●··●··●

JAMES THOMPSON fled from Maryland to take up an adventurous life at sea as a fugitive slave. He was whaling in the same oceans and at the same time as Herman Melville, although the two never met. This narrative is one of several which depict adventurous lives at sea and on the river while all of the narratives deal with the escapades of being a fugitive slave (1856 Worcester edition). "Uncle Tom's Bear Fight," another Alabama narrative from the WPA project, shows that the slave had to fear more than his master.

1

We cruised around the coast of Africa for whales, but finding none, put into the port of Johanna; where we again met the ship *Sally Ann*, Captain Burton, who had the reputation of being a very cruel man.

While lying in port, six or seven of his men, taking with them provisions, a compass, quadrant, chart, nautical almanac, spy glass, and other useful implements of navigation, one morning before daylight, took a boat and made off, intending to go to Mohilla, one of the Comoro Islands, about ten miles from Johanna. But before they were out of sight, they were discovered from the ship.

Now, there is a reef of rocks running about one and a half miles out to sea, from the port of Johanna, which are, at all times, very dangerous, in consequence of the heavy seas which are constantly breaking over them. When Captain Burton discovered and gave chase to his deserting crew, they ran at once among these reefs, and thus escaped, he not daring to follow them, but returning to his ship much fatigued and exasperated.

It seemed that the Johannicans and Mohillans had been at war with each other, and consequently no intercourse was permitted between the islands. Captain Burton offered the Johanna king a large reward, if he would catch his runaways, and deliver them up to him when he returned from a short cruise, which he was now obliged to make, and from which he should return in about three weeks. But the king, fearing to approach the shores of his enemy's island, only cruised about his own, and of course with no success; so he finally gave up the search, and the ship was obliged to put out to sea without them, though the captain swore he would have them, if they went to hell!

Five days afterwards they discovered a sperm whale, after which they immediately gave chase. He went down and finally came up very near the captain's boat, when he gave orders to harpoon him, which the boatsteerer immediately did, and fastened him. The captain then went forward to lance him, when the whale struck him so violent a blow with his tail, as to break both his legs, without injuring another person. He was taken directly to Johanna, but there being no surgeon there, he was obliged to remain in this painful situation until an English vessel having one on board, came into port. But by this time his limbs were so badly swollen, that one of them could not be properly set, so he was taken to Cape Town, from whence he was sent to America. Three of his runaway crew were taken on board a French vessel, nearly in a state of starvation, while the rest actually perished.

We lay in this port about a week. It is a very ancient town, the houses of one story, mostly built of stone, and seldom having any windows. The inhabitants are Arabs, Malays and Africans. They are of a light brown complexion, and have regular features. Their religion is Mahomedan, the rites of which they scrupulously observe. They are exceedingly jealous of their females, insomuch that they will not permit them to speak to any man, out of their own family circle. They wear sad countenances, but are very hospitable. They have large and splendidly decorated temples, the floors of which are covered with striped matting, of their own manufacture.

One of the natives, who seemed a man of some influence and high moral standing, one day invited me to visit, with him, one of these temples; which invitation I gladly accepted. When we reached the door, my conductor stopped to speak to a person who I supposed was a priest, as he sat by a table on which lay a book and many papers, from which he was reading in a tuneful voice. A stone trough was standing beside the church.

I bolted at once into the temple, without hesitation, but was as soon brought back and told that I had defiled it, in consequence of not purifying myself before entering. The priest seemed very much offended, but led me to the trough, in which was a constantly changing supply of clean, fresh water, and bade me wash my hands and feet before entering.

I was told that my sacrilegious entrance, unpurified,

would oblige them to perform an extra sacrifice, by way of atonement. I regretted much that I had unwittingly been the cause of so much trouble, and thought an acknowledgment a sufficient sacrifice, but I was mistaken.

After being properly prepared, I was allowed to enter and remain during their service. I was astonished at the reverence and humility with which they approached the throne of grace, for they fell flat upon their faces.

Many things might be said concerning the manners and customs prevalent on this Island, as also concerning its towns; but my business is to describe my voyage to the Indian Ocean, to which I will now return.

We left this Island, and sailed in the direction of New Zealand, near which we cruised five weeks, taking several whales in the time. Four other vessels were in company with us here, each of which went in for himself, taking whales.

During one of our whaling adventures, I unwillingly consented to accompany the mate, at his request. I attributed most of the accidents to his carelessness; notwithstanding, he was called a skillful whaleman, therefore I did not like to go with him. He would rush to attack a whale, like a restless horse to battle, harpooning him without any regard to order or formality, lest some other boat should secure him first. We here took three whales in one week.

We one day fell in with a ship from Sag Harbor, having on board the dead bodies of two men, the captain of which came on board the *Milwood*, one beautiful Sabbath morning, when the sea was as smooth as glass, to ask our captain and such of the crew as chose to accompany him, to go on board his ship and attend their funeral.

I went and witnessed what is, probably, one of the

most solemn and affecting of scenes,—a burial at sea. All who witnessed it were affected with sadness. When all was ready for the final ceremony, the bodies were taken to the waist gangway, where they were lashed upon boards, lying upon their backs, with heavy bags of sand attached to their feet, after which they were committed to the waves, and instantly sank into the vast deep. Captain Luce performed the religious services with great solemnity.

After cruising in these seas about two months, we put into a harbor on New Zealand, where we stayed one week, and then went to New Holland for the cure of the scurvy, with which the sailors were badly afflicted, in consequence of having been so long exposed to an atmosphere loaded with saline vapors, and of being so long fed upon salted food. Eating raw potatoes is considered by some an excellent remedy for this disease, which commences with an irruption of the skin, and ends in putrefaction, if not arrested in season to prevent.

Another remedy, and one to which our sailors were subjected, is reckoned very good, namely: to bury the patient in the ground, all but his head, for a while. After the diseased ones had thus been cured, we cruised for a long time with no success, and finally returned to the Crowsett Islands; but even here were unsuccessful.

We had now been at sea over two years, and had completed our cargo, all save 50 bbls., when our captain decided to cruise towards home, keeping up a sharp lookout, until we were beyond the whaling ground. This decision filled me with joy, for I yearned to see my long unseen family.

The captain said to me one day, when we had been sometime homeward bound, "Steward, I thought you promised us a full cargo to return with, which you see we have not got; so I must think you a hypocrite!" I told him I still believed my prayers would be answered, and that we should yet have a full cargo.

About two weeks after this, while the ship, with all her canvas spread, and with a fair wind, was running after the rate of nine knots an hour, the man aloft saw two whales in the distance. The captain had offered ten dollars for a whale that would furnish 50 bbls. of oil, and each man was desirous of winning the prize. Preparations were soon made to give chase to the whales, who were still at a considerable distance from the ship.

The mate's boat soon fastened one whale, but while the captain was striving to fasten the other, he stove the boat and tumbled the crew into the water. The mate's crew, however, after killing their whale, took after this, and finally secured him, while the second mate's boat picked up the almost despairing crew. The two whales filled 150 bbls. with oil, so that there was not place in the ship to stow it, without throwing over some of the provisions to make room. We then went into Soldonna for refreshment, and while there lost four of our crew by desertion.

We next stopped at St. Helena, which renowned place I was very glad to see, and took occasion to visit the residence and tomb of the Emperor Napoleon. But I discovered nothing very remarkable at either place, therefore will not weary my readers with unimportant description. After one week's stay we left St. Helena for the American coast.

About three days out from this island, we spoke a ship, recently from home, by which the captain learned that since he left home his wife had given birth to a son. This filled him with joy, and made him so anxious to reach home, that he ordered the mate to put the ship under all the sail which she would bear.

The wind blew so furiously that it sometimes seemed

as if the sails must all be carried away; but like a gallant bark, the ship safely outrode the whole, and arrived at New Bedford. No pilot being in sight, we had to fire twenty rounds from the cannon as a signal, before we could raise one. At last, however, to our great joy, a pilot boat hove in sight, dancing over the waves, when shouts were heard, "O, sir, we shall soon get into harbor!" Then the joyful hymn was sung:

> By faith I see the land,
> The port of endless rest;
> My soul, each sail expand,
> And fly to Jesus' breast.
> Oh! may I gain that heavenly shore,
> Where winds and waves disturb no more.

But our singing was soon turned into sighing, our joy into sadness, for our pilot, being unacquainted with the New Bedford channel, could only take us in sight of the city, where we were left nearly two days to brood over our bitter disappointment.

How often do professed ministers of the Christian Church pretend to lead the anxious soul to the haven of eternal rest, when they are themselves ignorant of the way, and of course leave him in the gulf of despair to mourn his sad disappointment. But the right pilot came at last and took us into New Bedford, and Oh, what joy filled my soul, when I was once more permitted to enter the congregation of the righteous, and to hear the sound of the Gospel Trumpet.

But my bliss was not complete, for I had a family in Philadelphia, whom I must hasten to see, that they might participate in my joy, and unite with me in praises to God for my safe preservation through so long a voyage; so, as soon as I received my wages, I left New Bedford. Before I left, the captain and mate both called to see me, the former giving me ten, and the latter five dollars, telling me to live faithful until death, and asking me to pray for them, which I promised to do, then bade them farewell, and left for Philadelphia.

JAMES THOMPSON

2

"Sho, I recollects about de slabery days," said uncle Tom as he whittled shavings from a soft piece of white pine. "I lived on a plantation down in Perry County an' I remembers a story bout somp'n dat happen to me a way back dar.

"I was a water boy for fifty fiel' han's dat worked in de sun all day long, an' I hadda carry many a bucket from de spring. It was a long walk one fiel' ober from where most of dem was workin'. De spring run down between some willow trees an' it was powerful cool down dere in de shade. I use' to lie on de moss an' let my bare belly git cool an' put my face in de outlet of de spring an' let de water trickle over my haid. Jus' about de time I gits a little rest one of dem niggers would call:

"'Water Boy! Bring dat bucket!' Den I grab up de bucket an' run back out in de hot sun.

"One day, on my las' trip, I was mighty tired an' I flop down on dat moss wid de sweat a-drippin' from my body, an' 'fore I knowed it I done fell slap to sleep. When I woke up, it was almost dark, an' I couldn't hear de slaves a-singin' in de fiel's, so I knowed dat dey had gone home. I shake my haid, an' look about me, an' my eyes came to res' on a little black bear cub a-drinkin' outen de spring. He so was a cute little boogar an' I made up my mind right den to try an' kotch him. I was jus' a little nigger 'bout ten year old an' didn't have no sense, but I sho' wanted dat little bear. He ain't seed me a-settin' dere, so I snuck up real cautious like, an' afore he knowed it I had dat little debil a-squealin' in my hands. I was jus' about to start home wid him, when I hears a rustlin' in de bushes an' afore I went ten feets, here come a big, black bear a-lopin' along right outen dem willow trees. I drop dat little critter 'caze I knowed dat was his mammy an' she was ravin' mad. When I let de little feller fall it must have hurt him somp'n awful caze he howl more dan eber, an' went a limpin' up to his mammy. Well, suh, dat ole woman she got so mad she made for me like two bolts of lightnin'. But dese here feets of mine begin a-doin' dere stuff. I knowed she was a-gainin' on me so I lets out a whoop for help. She chased me 'cross dat empty field an' 'bout dat time I seen Big Jim a-comin' through a row of corn.

" 'Hurry Big Jim,' I calls, 'a bear is after me!'

"Big Jim was de biggest nigger on our place. He must have weighed as much as a half a bale of cotton.

"I was jus' 'bout gittin' to de edge of de corn when dat bear catched me. She give me a slap wid her paw an' I goes down wid my mouth a-scoopin' up de dus'. My back felt like somebody done put a hot iron on it. Dat bear was a mean one. I was expectin' her to chaw me up an' I drawed my body up in a knot and kivered my haid wid my hands an' waited. But dat bear neber touch me agin'.

"I kinda snuck my eye aroun' an' I saw Big Jim havin' it out wid her. Jim, he had a long knife an' dey was a-tumblin' an' a-rollin' in de dust, while I sot dere wid my eyes a-poppin' outen my haid an' my back feelin' like it was broke. Jim he wrap his legs roun' dat bear an' 'fore you knowed it he had done stuck dat ole critter a dozen times wid dat knife.

"About fifteen minutes later me an' Jim was a-walkin' back through de corn fiel' an' I guess we looked a sight, 'caze I was all tore up an' Jim he looked like he done mess up wid a fambly of wildcats.

He was bleedin' from haid to foot. When we walked into de big house to git some treatments an' medicine for our hurts, Mistis was a-standin' dere. When she seed me an' Jim, she almost faint. She says: 'Whut done happen to my niggers?'

"Atter me an' Jim got fixed up I was jus' as happy, caze I done seed de bes' fight dere eber was, an' I had me a little orphan bear cub."

"UNCLE TOM'S BEAR FIGHT"

Revolt

●··●··●··●··●··●··●··●··●··●··●··●··●··●··●··●··●

In December 1831, fifty thousand copies of the *Confessions* of NAT TURNER were being sold out of Baltimore. The 1831 copy in the Schomburg Library is used here. Marion Starling refers to the "soundless clarity of the candid-camera flash" to be found in the description of the massacre of some fifty-one to fifty-five whites. The same author notes also how slave revolts were fanned during years of economic hardship for the whole nation. Starling's thesis quotes statistics showing forty-seven known slave revolts between 1741 and 1800 and two hundred and ten between 1791 and 1856. The HARRIET JACOBS extract (1861 Boston edition) throws an interesting light on the effects of the revolt for the rest of the slave community.

1

Agreeable to his own appointment, on the evening he was committed to prison, with permission of the jailer, I visited NAT on Tuesday the 1st November, when, without being questioned at all, he commenced his narrative in the following words:—

SIR,—You have asked me to give a history of the motives which induced me to undertake the late insurrection, as you call it—To do so I must go back to the days of my infancy, and even before I was born. I was thirty-one years of age the 2d of October last, and born the property of Benj. Turner, of this county. In my childhood a circumstance occurred which made an indelible impression on my mind, and laid the groundwork of that enthusiasm, which has terminated so fatally to many, both white and black, and for which I am about to atone at the gallows. It is here necessary to relate this circumstance—trifling as it may seem, it was the commencement of that belief which has grown with time, and even now, sir, in this dungeon, helpless and forsaken as I am, I cannot divest myself of. Being at play with other children, when three or four years old, I was telling them something, which my mother overhearing, said it had happened before I was born—I stuck by my story, however, and related some things which went, in her opinion, to confirm it—others being called on were greatly astonished, knowing that these things had happened, and caused them to say in my hearing, I surely would be a prophet, as the Lord had shewn me things that had happened before my birth. And my father and mother strengthened me in this my first impression, saying in my presence, I was intended for some great purpose, which they had always thought from certain marks on my head and breast—[a parcel of excrescences which I believe are not at all uncommon, particularly among negroes, as I have seen several with the same. In this case he has either cut them off or they have nearly disappeared]—My grandmother, who was very religious, to whom I was much attached—my master, who belonged to the church, and other religious persons who visited the house, and whom I often saw at prayers, noticing the singularity of my manners, I suppose, and my uncommon intelligence for a child, remarked I had too much sense to be raised, and if I was, I would never be of any service to any one as a slave—To a mind like mine, restless, inquisitive and observant of every thing that was passing, it is easy to suppose that religion was the subject to which it would be directed, and although this subject principally occupied my thoughts—there was nothing that I saw or heard of to which my attention was not directed—The manner in which I learned to read and write, not only had great influence on my mind, as I acquired it with the most perfect ease, so much so, that I have no recollection whatever of learning the alphabet—but to the astonishment of the family, one day, when a book was shewn me to keep me from crying, I began spelling the names of different objects—this was a source of wonder to all in the neighborhood, particularly the blacks—and this learning was constantly improved at all opportunities—when I got large enough to go to work, while employed, I was reflecting on many things that would present themselves to my imagination, and whenever an opportunity occurred of looking at a book, when the school children were getting their lessons, I would find many things that the fertility of my own imagination had depicted to me before; all my time, not devoted to my master's service, was spent either in prayer, or in making experiments in casting different things in moulds made of earth, in attempting to make paper, gunpowder, and many other experiments, that although I could not perfect, yet convinced me of its practicability if I had the means.* I was not addicted to stealing in my youth, nor have ever been—Yet such was the confidence of the negroes in the neighborhood, even at this early period of my life, in my superior judgment,

* When questioned as to the manner of manufacturing those different articles, he was found well informed on the subject.

that they would often carry me with them when they
were going on any roguery, to plan for them. Grow-
ing up among them, with the confidence in my superior judgment, and when this, in their opinions,
was perfected by Divine inspiration, from the circumstances already alluded to in my infancy, and which
belief was ever afterwards zealously inculcated by
the austerity of my life and manners, which became
the subject of remark by white and black.—Having
soon discovered to be great, I must appear so, and
therefore studiously avoided mixing in society, and
wrapped myself in mystery, devoting my time to fasting and prayer—By this time, having arrived to man's
estate, and hearing the scriptures commented on at
meetings, I was struck with that particular passage
which says: "Seek ye the kingdom of Heaven and all
things shall be added unto you." I reflected much on
this passage, and prayed daily for light on this subject
—As I was praying one day at my plough, the spirit
spoke to me, saying "Seek ye the kingdom of Heaven
and all things shall be added unto you." QUESTION—
What do you mean by the spirit? ANSWER. The Spirit
that spoke to the prophets in former days—and I was
greatly astonished, and for two years prayed continually, whenever my duty would permit—and then again
I had the same revelation, which fully confirmed me
in the impression that I was ordained for some great
purpose, in the hands of the Almighty. Several years
rolled round, in which many events occurred to
strengthen me in this my belief. At this time I re-
verted in my mind to the remarks made of me in my
childhood, and the things that had been shewn me—
and as it had been said of me in my childhood by
those by whom I had been taught to pray, both white
and black, and in whom I had the greatest confidence,
that I had too much sense to be raised, and if I was, I
would never be of any use to anyone as a slave. Now

finding I had arrived to man's estate, and was a slave, and these revelations being made known to me, I began to direct my attention to this great object, to fulfil the purpose for which, by this time, I felt assured I was intended. Knowing the influence I had obtained over the minds of my fellow servants, (not by the means of conjuring and such like tricks—for to them I always spoke of such things with contempt) but by the communion of the Spirit whose revelations I often communicated to them, and they believed and said my wisdom came from God. I now began to prepare them for my purpose, by telling them something was about to happen that would terminate in fulfilling the great promise that had been made to me—About this time I was placed under an overseer, from whom I ran away—and after remaining in the woods thirty days, I returned, to the astonishment of the negroes on the plantation, who thought I had made my escape to some other part of the country, as my father had done before. But the reason of my return was, that the Spirit appeared to me and said I had my wishes directed to the things of this world, and not to the kingdom of Heaven, and that I should return to the service of my earthly master—"For he who knoweth his Master's will, and doeth it not, shall be beaten with many stripes, and thus have I chastened you." And the negroes found fault, and murmured against me, saying that if they had my sense they would not serve any master in the world. And about this time I had a vision—and I saw white spirits and black spirits engaged in battle, and the sun was darkened—the thunder rolled in the Heavens, and blood flowed in streams —and I heard a voice saying, "Such is your luck, such you are called to see, and let it come rough or smooth, you must surely bare it." I now withdrew myself as much as my situation would permit, from the intercourse of my fellow servants, for the avowed purpose of serving the Spirit more fully—and it appeared to me, and reminded me of the things it had already shown me, and that it would then reveal to me the knowledge of the elements, the revolution of the planets, the operation of tides, and changes of the seasons. After the revelation in the year 1825, and the knowledge of the elements being made known to me, I sought more than ever to obtain true holiness before the great day of judgment should appear, and then I began to receive the true knowledge of faith. And from the first steps of righteousness until the last, was I made perfect; and the Holy Ghost was with me, and said, "Behold me as I stand in the Heavens"— and I looked and saw the forms of men in different attitudes—and there were lights in the sky to which the children of darkness gave other names than what they really were—for they were lights of the Saviour's hands, stretched forth from east to west, even as they were extended on the cross on Calvary for the redemption of sinners. And I wondered greatly at these miracles, and prayed to be informed of a certainty of the meaning thereof—and shortly afterwards, while laboring in the field, I discovered drops of blood on the corn as though it were drew from heaven—and I communicated it to many, both white and black, in the neighborhood—and I then found on the leaves in the woods hieroglyphic characters, and numbers, with the forms of men in different attitudes, portrayed in blood, and representing the figures I had seen before in the heavens. And now the Holy Ghost had revealed itself to me, and made plain the miracles it had shown me— For as the blood of Christ has been shed on this earth, and had ascended to heaven for the salvation of sinners, and now was returning to earth again in the form of dew—and as the leaves on the trees bore the impression of the figures I had seen in the heavens, it was plain to me that the Saviour was about to lay down the yoke he had borne for the sins of men, and the great day of judgment was at hand. About this time I told these things to a white man, (Etheldred T. Brantley) on whom it had a wonderful effect—and he ceased from his wickedness, and was attacked immediately with a cutaneous eruption, and blood oozed from the pores of his skin, and after praying and fasting nine days, he was healed, and the Spirit appeared to me again, and said, as the Saviour had been baptised so should we be also—and when the white people would not let us be baptised by the church, we went down into the water together, in the sight of many who reviled us, and were baptised by the Spirit—After this I rejoiced greatly, and gave thanks to God. And on the 12th of May, 1828, I heard a loud noise in the heavens, and the Spirit instantly appeared to me and said the Serpent was loosened, and Christ had laid down the yoke he had borne for the sins of men, and that I should take it on and fight against the Serpent, for the time was fast approaching when the first should be last and the last should be first. QUESTION. Do you not find yourself mistaken now? ANSWER. Was not Christ crucified? And by signs in the heavens that it would be made known to me when I should commence the great work—and until the first sign appeared, I should conceal it from the knowledge of men—And on the appearance of the sign, (the eclipse of the sun last February) I should arise and prepare myself, and slay my enemies with their own weapons. And immediately on the sign appearing in the heavens, the seal was removed from my lips, and I communicated the great work laid out before me to do, to four in whom I had the greatest confidence, (Henry, Hark, Nelson, and Sam)—It was intended by us to have begun the work of death on the 4th of July last—Many were the plans formed and rejected by us, and it affected my mind to such a degree, that I fell sick, and the time passed without our coming to any determination how to commence— Still forming new schemes and rejecting them, when the sign appeared again, which determined me not to wait longer.

Since the commencement of 1830, I had been living with Mr. Joseph Travis, who was to me a kind master, and placed the greatest confidence in me; in fact, I had no cause to complain of his treatment of me. On Saturday evening, the 20th of August, it was agreed between Henry, Hark and myself, to prepare a dinner the next day for the men we expected, and then to concert a plan, as we had not yet determined on any. Hark, on the following morning, brought a pig, and Henry brandy, and being joined by Sam, Nelson, Will and Jack, they prepared in the woods a dinner, where, about three o'clock, I joined them.

QUESTION. Why were you so backward in joining them?

ANSWER. The same reason that had caused me not to mix with them for years before.

I saluted them on coming up, and asked Will how came he there, he answered, his life was worth no more than others, and his liberty as dear to him. I asked him if he thought to obtain it? He said he would, or lose his life. This was enough to put him in full confidence. Jack, I knew, was only a tool in the hands of Hark, it was quickly agreed we should commence at home (Mr. J. Travis') on that night, and until we had armed and equipped ourselves, and gathered sufficient force, neither age nor sex was to be spared, (which was invariably adhered to). We remained at the feast, until about two hours in the night, when we went to the house and found Austin; they all went to the cider press and drank, except myself. On returning to the house Hark went to the door with an axe, for the purpose of breaking it open, as we knew we were strong enough to murder the family, if they were awakened by the noise; but reflecting that it might create an alarm in the neighborhood, we determined to enter the house secretly, and murder them whilst sleeping. Hark got a ladder and set it against the chimney, on which I ascended, and hoisting a window, entered and came down stairs, unbarred the door, and removed the guns from their places. It was then observed that I must spill the first blood. On which, armed with a hatchet, and accompanied by Will, I entered my master's chamber, it being dark, I could not give a death blow, the hatched glanced from his head, he sprang from the bed and called his wife, it was his last word, Will laid him dead, with a blow of his axe, and Mrs. Travis shared the same fate, as she lay in bed. The murder of this family, five in number, was the work of a moment, not one of them awoke; there was a little infant sleeping in a cradle, that was forgotten, until we had left the house and gone some distance, when Henry and Will returned and killed it; we got here, four guns that would shoot, and several old muskets, with a pound or two of powder. We remained some time at the barn, where we paraded; I formed them in a line as soldiers, and after carrying them through all the manoeuvres I was master of, marched them off to Mr. Salathul Francis', about six hundred yards distant. Sam and Will went to the door and knocked. Mr. Francis asked who was there, Sam replied it was him, and he had a letter for him, on which he got up and came to the door; they immediately seized him, and dragging him out a little from the door, he was dispatched by repeated blows on the head; there was no other white person in the family. We started from there for Mrs. Reese's, maintaining the most perfect silence on our march, where finding the door unlocked, we entered, and murdered Mrs. Reese in her bed, while sleeping; her son awoke, but it was only to sleep the sleep of

death, he had only time to say who is that, and he
was no more. From Mrs. Reese's we went to Mrs. Turner's, a mile distant, which we reached about sunrise,
on Monday morning. Henry, Austin, and Sam, went to
the still, where, finding Mr. Peebles, Austin shot him,
and the rest of us went to the house; as we approached,
the family discovered us, and shut the door. Vain hope!
Will, with one stroke of his axe opened it, and we entered and found Mrs. Turner and Mrs. Newsome in the
middle of a room, almost frightened to death. Will
immediately killed Mrs. Turner, with one blow of his
axe. I took Mrs. Newsome by the hand, and with the
sword I had when I was apprehended, I struck her
several blows over the head, but not being able to kill
her, as the sword was dull. Will turning around and
discovering it, dispatched her also. A general destruction of property and search for money and ammunition, always succeeded the murders. By this time my
company amounted to fifteen, and nine men mounted,
who started for Mrs. Whitehead's, (the other six were
to go through a byway to Mr. Bryant's, and rejoin
us at Mrs. Whitehead's,) as we approached the house
we discovered Mr. Richard Whitehead standing in the
cotton patch, near the lane fence; we called him over
into the lane, and Will, the executioner, was near at
hand, with his fatal axe, to send him to an untimely
grave. As we pushed on to the house, I discovered
some one run round the garden, and thinking it was
some of the white family, I pursued them, but finding
it was a servant girl belonging to the house, I returned to commence the work of death, but they
whom I left, had not been idle; all the family were
already murdered, but Mrs. Whitehead and her daughter Margaret. As I came around to the door I saw Will
pulling Mrs. Whitehead out of the house, and at the
step he nearly severed her head from her body, with
his broad axe. Miss Margaret, when I discovered her,

had concealed herself in the corner, formed by the projection of the cellar cap from the house; on my approach she fled, but was soon overtaken, and after repeated blows with a sword, I killed her by a blow on the head, with a fence rail. By this time, the six who had gone by Mr. Bryant's, rejoined us, and informed me they had done the work of death assigned them. We again divided, part going to Mr. Richard Porter's, and from thence to Nathaniel Francis', the others to Mr. Howell Harris', and Mr. T. Doyle's. On my reaching Mr. Porter's, he had escaped with his family. I understood there, that the alarm had already spread, and I immediately returned to bring up those sent to Mr. Doyle's and Mr. Harris'; the party I left going on to Mr. Francis', having told them I would join them in that neighborhood. I met those sent to Mr. Doyle's and Mr. Harris' returning, having met Mr. Doyle on the road and killed him; and learning from some who joined them, that Mr. Harris was from home, I immediately pursued the course taken by the party gone on before; but knowing they would complete the work of death and pillage, at Mr. Francis' before I could get there, I went on to Mr. Peter Edwards', expecting to find them there, but they had been here also. I then went to Mr. John T. Barrow's, they had been here and murdered him. I pursued on their track to Capt. Newit Harris', where I found the greater part mounted, and ready to start; the men now amounting to about forty, shouted and hurrahed as I rode up, some were in the yard, loading their guns, others drinking. They said Captain Harris and his family had escaped, the property in the house they destroyed, robbing him of money and other valuables. I ordered them to mount and march instantly, this was about nine or ten o'clock, Monday morning. I proceeded to Mr. Levi Waller's, two or three miles distant. I took my station in the rear, as it 'twas my object to carry terror and devastation wherever we went, I placed fifteen or twenty of the best armed and most to be relied on, in front, who generally approached the houses as fast as their horses could run; this was for two purposes, to prevent their escape and strike terror to the inhabitants —on this account I never got to the houses, after leaving Mrs. Whitehead's, until the murders were committed, except in one case. I sometimes got in sight in time to see the work of death completed, viewed the mangled bodies as they lay, in silent satisfaction, and immediately started in quest of other victims— Having murdered Mrs. Waller and ten children, we started for Mr. William Williams'—having killed him and two little boys that were there; while engaged in this, Mrs. Williams fled and got some distance from the house, but she was pursued, overtaken, and compelled to get up behind one of the company, who brought her back, and after showing her the mangled body of her lifeless husband, she was told to get down and lay by his side, where she was shot dead. I then started for Mr. Jacob Williams', where the family were murdered—Here we found a young man named Drury, who had come on business with Mr. Williams— he was pursued, overtaken and shot. Mrs. Vaughan was the next place visited—and after murdering the family here, I determined on starting for Jerusalem—Our number amounted now to fifty or sixty, all mounted and armed with guns, axes, swords and clubs—On reaching Mr. James W. Parker's gate, immediately on the road leading to Jerusalem, and about three miles distant, it was proposed to me to call there, but I objected, as I knew he was gone to Jerusalem, and my object was to reach there as soon as possible; but some of the men having relations at Mr. Parker's it was agreed that they might call and get his people. I remained at the gate on the road, with seven or eight; the others going across the field to the house, about half a mile off. After waiting some time for them, I became impatient, and started to the house for them, and on our return we were met by a party of white men, who had pursued our blood-stained track, and who had fired on those at the gate, and dispersed them, which I knew nothing of, not having been at that time rejoined by any of them—Immediately on discovering the whites, I ordered my men to halt and form, as they appeared to be alarmed—The white men, eighteen in number, approached us in about one hundred yards, when one of them fired, (this was against the positive orders of Captain Alexander P. Peete, who commanded, and who had directed the men to reserve their fire until within thirty paces) And I discovered about half of them retreating, I then ordered my men to fire and rush them; the few remaining stood their ground until we approached within fifty yards, when they fired and retreated. We pursued and overtook some of them who we thought we left dead; (they were not killed) after pursuing them about two hundred yards, and rising a little hill, I discovered they were met by another party, and had halted, and were re-loading their guns, (this was a small party from Jerusalem who knew the negroes were in the field, and had just tied their horses to wait their return to the road, knowing that Mr. Parker and family were in Jerusalem, but knew nothing of the party that had gone in with Captain Peete; on hearing the firing they immediately rushed to the spot and arrived just in time to arrest the progress of these barbarous villains, and save the lives of their friends and fellow citizens). Thinking that those who retreated first, and the party who fired on us at fifty or sixty yards distant, had all only fallen back to meet others with ammunition. As I saw them re-loading their guns, and more coming up than I saw at first, and several of my bravest men being wounded, the others became panick

struck and squandered over the field; the white men
pursued and fired on us several times. Hark had his
horse shot under him, and I caught another for him as
it was running by me; five or six of my men were
wounded, but none left on the field; finding myself de-
feated here I instantly determined to go through a private way, and cross the Nottoway river at the Cypress
Bridge, three miles below Jerusalem, and attack that
place in the rear, as I expected they would look for
me on the other road, and I had a great desire to get
there to procure arms and ammunition. After going a
short distance in this private way, accompanied by
about twenty men, I overtook two or three who told
me the others were dispersed in every direction. After
trying in vain to collect a sufficient force to proceed to
Jerusalem, I determined to return, as I was sure they
would take back to their old neighborhood, where
they would join me, make new recruits, and come
down again. On my way back, I called at Mrs.
Thomas's, Mr. Spencer's, and several other places,
the white families having fled, we found no more victims to gratify our thirst for blood, we stopped at
Majr. Ridley's quarter for the night, and being joined
by four of his men, with the recruits made since my
defeat, we mustered now about forty strong. After
placing our sentinels, I laid down to sleep, but was
quickly roused by a great racket; starting up, I found
some mounted, and others in great confusion; one of
the sentinels having given the alarm that we were
about to be attacked, I ordered some to ride round
and reconnoitre, and on their return the others being
more alarmed, not knowing who they were, fled in
different ways, so that I was reduced to about twenty
again; with this I determined to attempt to recruit,
and proceed on to rally in the neighborhood, I had
left. Dr. Blunt's was the nearest house, which we
reached just before day; on riding up the yard, Hark

fired a gun. We expected Dr. Blunt and his family were at Maj. Ridley's, as I knew there was a company of men there; the gun was fired to ascertain if any of the family were at home; we were immediately fired upon and retreated, leaving several of my men. I do not know what became of them, as I never saw them afterwards. Pursuing our course back and coming in sight of Captain Harris', where we had been the day before, we discovered a party of white men at the house, on which all deserted me but two, (Jacob and Nat,) we concealed ourselves in the woods until near night, when I sent them in search of Henry, Sam, Nelson, and Hark, and directed them to rally all they could, at the place we had had our dinner the Sunday before, where they would find me, and I accordingly returned there as soon as it was dark and remained until Wednesday evening, when discovering white men riding around the place as though they were looking for some one, and none of my men joining me, I concluded Jacob and Nat had been taken, and compelled to betray me. On this I gave up all hope for the present; and on Thursday night after having supplied myself with provisions from Mr. Travis' I scratched a hole under a pile of fence rails in a field, where I concealed myself for six weeks, never leaving my hiding place but for a few minutes in the dead of night to get water which was very near; thinking by this time I could venture out, I began to go about in the night and eavesdrop the houses in the neighborhood; pursuing this course for about a fortnight and gathering little or no intelligence, afraid of speaking to any human being, and returning every morning to my cave before dawn of day. I know not how long I might have led this life, if accident had not betrayed me, a dog in the neighborhood passing by my hiding place one night while I was out, was attracted by some meat I had in my cave, and crawled in and stole it, and was coming out just as I returned. A few nights after, two negroes having started to go hunting with the same dog, and passed that way, the dog came again to the place, and having just gone out to walk about, discovered me and barked, on which thinking myself discovered, I spoke to them to beg concealment. On making myself known they fled from me. Knowing then they would betray me, I immediately left my hiding place, and was pursued almost incessantly until I was taken a fortnight afterwards by Mr. Benjamin Phipps, in a little hole I had dug out with my sword, for the purpose of concealment, under the top of a fallen tree. On Mr. Phipps' discovering the place of my concealment, he cocked his gun and aimed at me. I requested him not to shoot and I would give up, upon which he demanded my sword. I delivered it to him, and he brought me to prison. During the time I was pursued, I had many hair breadth escapes, which your time will not permit you to relate. I am here loaded with chains, and willing to suffer the fate that awaits me.

I here proceeded to make some inquiries of him, after assuring him of certain death that awaited him, and that concealment would only bring destruction on the innocent as well as the guilty, of his own color, if he knew of any extensive or concerted plan. His answer was, I do not. When I questioned him as to the insurrection in North Carolina happening about the same time, he denied any knowledge of it; and when I looked him in the face as though I would search his inmost thoughts, he replied, "I see sir, you doubt my word; but can you not think the same ideas, and strange appearances about this time in the heaven's might prompt others, as well as myself, to this undertaking." I now had much conversation with and asked him many questions, having forborne to do so previously, except in the cases noted in parenthesis; but during his statement, I had, unnoticed by him, taken notes as to some particular circumstances, and having the advantage of his statement before me in writing, on the evening of the third day that I had been with him, I began a cross examination, and found his statement corroborated by every circumstance coming within my own knowledge of the confessions of others whom had been either killed or executed, and whom he had not seen nor had any knowledge since 22d of August last, he expressed himself fully satisfied as to the impracticability of his attempt. It has been said he was ignorant and cowardly, and that his object was to murder and rob for the purpose of obtaining money to make his escape. It is notorious, that he was never known to have a dollar in his life; to swear an oath, or drink a drop of spirits. As to his ignorance, he certainly never had the advantages of education, but he can read and write, (it was taught him by his parents,) and for natural intelligence and quickness of apprehension, is surpassed by few men I have ever seen. As to his being a coward, his reason as given for not resisting Mr. Phipps, shews the decision of his character. When he saw Mr. Phipps present his gun, he said he knew it was impossible for him to escape as the woods were full of men; he therefore thought it was better to surrender, and trust to fortune for his escape. He is a complete fanatic, or plays his part most admirably. On other subjects he possesses an uncommon share of intelligence, with a mind capable of attaining anything; but warped and perverted by the influence of early impressions. He is below the ordinary stature, though strong and active, having the true negro face, every feature of which is strongly marked. I shall not attempt to describe the effect of his narrative, as told and commented on by himself, in the condemned hole of the prison. The calm, deliberate composure with which he spoke of his late deeds and intentions, the expression of his fiend-like face when excited by enthusiasm, still bearing the stains of blood of helpless innocence about him; clothed with rags and covered with chains; yet daring to raise his manacled hands to heaven, with a spirit soaring above the attributes of man; I looked on him and my blood curdled in my veins.

I will not shock the feelings of humanity, nor wound afresh the bosoms of the disconsolate sufferers in this unparalleled and inhuman massacre, by detailing the deeds of their fiend-like barbarity. There were two or three who were in the power of these wretches, had they known it, and who escaped in the most providential manner. There were two whom they thought they left dead on the field at Mr. Parker's, but who were only stunned by the blows of their guns, as they did not take time to re-load when they charged on them. The escape of a little girl who went to school at Mr. Waller's, and where the children were collecting for that purpose, excited general sympathy. As their teacher had not arrived, they were at play in the yard, and seeing the negroes approach, she ran up on a dirt chimney, (such as are common to log houses,) and remained there unnoticed during the massacre of the eleven that were killed at this place. She remained on her hiding place till just before the arrival of a party, who were in pursuit of the murderers, when she came down and fled to a swamp, where, a mere child as she was, with the horrors of the late scene before her, she lay concealed until the next day, when seeing a party go up to the house, she came up, and on being asked how she escaped, replied with the utmost simplicity, "The Lord helped her." She was taken up behind a gentleman of the party, and returned to the arms of her weeping mother. Miss Whitehead concealed herself between the bed and the mat that supported it, while they murdered her sister in the

same room, without discovering her. She was afterwards carried off, and concealed for protection by a
slave of the family, who gave evidence against several
of them on their trial. Mrs. Nathaniel Francis, while
concealed in a closet heard their blows, and the shrieks
of the victims of these ruthless savages; they then entered the closet where she was concealed, and went
out without discovering her. While in this hiding place,
she heard two of her women in a quarrel about the
division of her clothes. Mr. John T. Baron, discovering
them approaching his house, told his wife to make
her escape, and scorning to fly, fell fighting on his own
threshold. After firing his rifle, he discharged his gun
at them, and then broke it over the villian who first
approached him, but he was overpowered, and slain.
His bravery, however, saved from the hands of these
monsters, his lovely and amiable wife, who will long
lament a husband so deserving of her love. As directed
by him, she attempted to escape through the garden,
when she was caught and held by one of her servant
girls, but another coming to her rescue, she fled to
the woods, and concealed herself. Few indeed; were
those who escaped their work of death. But fortunate for society, the hand of retributive justice has
overtaken them; and not one that was known to be
concerned has escaped.

NAT TURNER

2

Not far from this time Nat Turner's insurrection broke
out; and the news threw our town into great commo-
tion. Strange that they should be alarmed, when their
slaves were so "contented and happy"! But so it was.

It was always the custom to have a muster every
year. On that occasion every white man shouldered

his musket. The citizens and the so-called country gentlemen wore military uniforms. The poor whites took
their places in the ranks in everyday dress, some without shoes, some without hats. This grand occasion had
already passed; and when the slaves were told there
was to be another muster, they were surprised and rejoiced. Poor creatures! They thought it was going to
be a holiday. I was informed of the true state of
affairs, and imparted it to the few I could trust.
Most gladly would I have proclaimed it to every slave;
but I dared not. All could not be relied on. Mighty
is the power of the torturing lash.

By sunrise, people were pouring in from every quarter within twenty miles of the town. I knew the houses
were to be searched; and I expected it would be done
by country bullies and the poor whites. I knew nothing annoyed them so much as to see colored people
living in comfort and respectability; so I made arrangements for them with especial care. I arranged
every thing in my grandmother's house as neatly as
possible. I put white quilts on the beds, and decorated
some of the rooms with flowers. When all was arranged, I sat down at the window to watch. Far as
my eye could reach, it rested on a motley crowd of
soldiers. Drums and fifes were discoursing martial
music. The men were divided into companies of sixteen, each headed by a captain. Orders were given,
and the wild scouts rushed in every direction, wherever a colored face was to be found.

It was a grand opportunity for the low whites, who
had no negroes of their own to scourge. They exulted
in such a chance to exercise a little brief authority,
and show their subserviency to the slaveholders; not
reflecting that the power which trampled on the colored people also kept themselves in poverty, ignorance,
and moral degradation. Those who never witnessed
such scenes can hardly believe what I know was in-

flicted at this time on innocent men, women, and children, against whom there was not the slightest ground for suspicion. Colored people and slaves who lived in remote parts of the town suffered in an especial manner. In some cases the searchers scattered powder and shot among their clothes, and then sent other parties to find them, and bring them forward as proof that they were plotting insurrection. Every where men, women, and children were whipped till the blood stood in puddles at their feet. Some received five hundred lashes; others were tied hands and feet, and tortured with a bucking paddle, which blisters the skin terribly. The dwellings of the colored people, unless they happened to be protected by some influential white person, who was nigh at hand, were robbed of clothing and every thing else the marauders thought worth carrying away. All day long these unfeeling wretches went round, like a troop of demons, terrifying and tormenting the helpless. At night, they formed themselves into patrol bands, and went wherever they chose among the colored people, acting out their brutal will. Many women hid themselves in woods and swamps, to keep out of their way. If any of the husbands or fathers told of these outrages, they were tied up to the public whipping post, and cruelly scourged for telling lies about white men. The consternation was universal. No two people that had the slightest tinge of color in their faces dared to be seen talking together.

I entertained no positive fears about our household, because we were in the midst of white families who would protect us. We were ready to receive the soldiers whenever they came. It was not long before we heard the tramp of feet and the sound of voices. The door was rudely pushed open; and in they tumbled, like a pack of hungry wolves. They snatched at every thing within their reach. Every box, trunk,

closet, and corner underwent a thorough examination.
A box in one of the drawers containing some silver
change was eagerly pounced upon. When I stepped
forward to take it from them, one of the soldiers
turned and said angrily, "What d'ye foller us fur? D'ye
s'pose white folks is come to steal?"

I replied, "You have come to search; but you have
searched that box, and I will take it, if you please."

At that moment I saw a white gentleman who was
friendly to us; and I called to him, and asked him to
have the goodness to come in and stay till the search
was over. He readily complied. His entrance into the
house brought in the captain of the company, whose
business it was to guard the outside of the house, and
see that none of the inmates left it. This officer was
Mr. Litch, the wealthy slaveholder whom I mentioned,
in the account of neighboring planters, as being notorious for his cruelty. He felt above soiling his hands
with the search. He merely gave orders; and, if a bit
of writing was discovered, it was carried to him by his
ignorant followers, who were unable to read.

My grandmother had a large trunk of bedding and
table cloths. When that was opened, there was a great
shout of surprise; and one exclaimed, "Where'd the
damned niggers git all dis sheet an' table clarf?"

My grandmother, emboldened by the presence of
our white protector, said, "You may be sure we didn't
pilfer 'em from *your* houses."

"Look here, mammy," said a grim-looking fellow
without any coat, "you seem to feel mighty gran' 'cause
you got all them 'ere fixens. White folks oughter have
'em all."

His remarks were interrupted by a chorus of voices
shouting, "We's got 'em! We's got 'em! Dis 'ere yaller
gal's got letters!"

There was a general rush for the supposed letter,
which, upon examination, proved to be some verses

written to me by a friend. In packing away my things, I had overlooked them. When their captain informed them of their contents, they seemed much disappointed. He inquired of me who wrote them. I told him it was one of my friends. "Can you read them?" he asked. When I told him I could, he swore, and raved, and tore the paper into bits. "Bring me all your letters!" said he, in a commanding tone. I told him I had none. "Don't be afraid," he continued, in an insinuating way. "Bring them all to me. Nobody shall do you any harm." Seeing I did not move to obey him, his pleasant tone changed to oaths and threats. "Who writes to you? half free niggers?" inquired he. I replied, "O, no; most of my letters are from white people. Some request me to burn them after they are read, and some I destroy without reading."

An exclamation of surprise from some of the company put a stop to our conversation. Some silver spoons which ornamented an old-fashioned buffet had just been discovered. My grandmother was in the habit of preserving fruit for many ladies in the town, and of preparing suppers for parties; consequently she had many jars of preserves. The closet that contained these was next invaded, and the contents tasted. One of them, who was helping himself freely, tapped his neighbor on the shoulder, and said, "Wal done! Don't wonder de niggers want to kill all de white folks, when dey live on 'sarves" [meaning preserves]. I stretched out my hand to take the jar, saying, "You were not sent here to search for sweetmeats."

"And what *were* we sent for?" said the captain, bristling up to me. I evaded the question.

The search of the house was completed, and nothing found to condemn us. They next proceeded to the garden, and knocked about every bush and vine, with no better success. The captain called his men together, and, after a short consultation, the order to march was given. As they passed out of the gate, the captain turned back, and pronounced a malediction on the house. He said it ought to be burned to the ground, and each of its inmates receive thirty-nine lashes. We came out of this affair very fortunately; not losing anything except some wearing apparel.

Towards evening the turbulence increased. The soldiers, stimulated by drink, committed still greater cruelties. Shrieks and shouts continually rent the air. Not daring to go to the door, I peeped under the window curtain. I saw a mob dragging along a number of colored people, each white man, with his musket upraised, threatening instant death if they did not stop their shrieks. Among the prisoners was a respectable old colored minister. They had found a few parcels of shot in his house, which his wife had for years used to balance her scales. For this they were going to shoot him on Court House Green. What a spectacle was that for a civilized country! A rabble, staggering under intoxication, assuming to be the administrators of justice!

The better class of the community exerted their influence to save the innocent, persecuted people; and in several instances they succeeded, by keeping them shut up in jail till the excitement abated. At last the white citizens found that their own property was not safe from the lawless rabble they had summoned to protect them. They rallied the drunken swarm, drove them back into the country, and set a guard over the town.

The next day, the town patrols were commissioned to search colored people that lived out of the city; and the most shocking outrages were committed with perfect impunity. Every day for a fortnight, if I looked out, I saw horsemen with some poor panting negro tied to their saddles, and compelled by the lash to keep up with their speed, till they arrived at the jail yard. Those who had been whipped too unmercifully to walk were washed with brine, tossed into a cart, and carried to jail. One black man, who had not fortitude to endure scourging, promised to give information about the conspiracy. But it turned out that he knew nothing at all. He had not even heard the name of Nat Turner. The poor fellow had, however, made up a story, which augmented his own sufferings and those of the colored people.

The day patrol continued for some weeks, and at sundown a night guard was substituted. Nothing at all was proved against the colored people, bond or free. The wrath of the slaveholders was somewhat appeased by the capture of Nat Turner. The imprisoned were released. The slaves were sent to their masters, and the free were permitted to return to their ravaged homes. Visiting was strictly forbidden on the plantations. The slaves begged the privilege of again meeting at their little church in the woods, with their burying ground around it. It was built by the colored people, and they had no higher happiness than to meet there and sing hymns together, and pour out their hearts in spontaneous prayer. Their request was denied, and the church was demolished. They were permitted to attend the white churches, a certain portion of the galleries being appropriated to their use. There, when everybody else had partaken of the communion, and the benediction had been pronounced, the minister said, "Come down, now, my colored friends." They obeyed the summons, and partook of the bread and wine, in commemoration of the meek and lowly Jesus, who said, "God is your Father, and all ye are brethren."

HARRIET JACOBS

Escape

●··●··●··●··●··●··●··●··●··●··●··●··●··●··●··●··●··●··●

HENRY "BOX" BROWN's narrative is one of the most startling ever written. He was, however, far from being the
only one to attempt escape trussed up in a box. Starling's
long list of recorded instances includes that of the unfortunate girl who contracted brain fever inside her box, only to
emerge gray-haired and permanently ten years older (1849
edition). JAMES W. C. PENNINGTON was a respected pastor
of a Presbyterian church in New York City. He was a Ph.D.
of the University of Heidelberg, a scholar who had to stand
outside the lecture rooms at Yale University to attend class.
On the eve of the disclosure that he was a fugitive slave,
he fled to England—to raise money to pay for his freedom
(1849 first edition).

1

I went to Mr. Allen, and requested of him permission
to refrain from labor for a short time, in consequence
of a disabled finger; but he refused to grant me this
permission, on the ground that my hand was not lame

enough to justify him in so doing. Nothing daunted by this rebuff, I took some oil of vitriol, intending to pour a few drops upon my finger, to make it sufficiently sore, to disable me from work, which I succeeded in, beyond my wishes; for in my hurry, a larger quantity than it was my purpose to apply to my finger, found its way there, and my finger was soon eaten through to the bone. The overseer then was obliged to allow me to absent myself from business, for it was impossible for me to work in that situation. But I did not waste my precious furlough in idle mourning over my fate. I armed myself with determined energy, for action, and in the words of one of old, in the name of God, "I leaped over a wall, and run through a troop" of difficulties. After searching for assistance for some time, I at length was so fortunate as to find a friend, who promised to assist me, for one half the money I had about me, which was one hundred and sixty-six dollars. I gave him eighty-six, and he was to do his best in forwarding my scheme. Long did we remain together, attempting to devise ways and means to carry me away from the land of separation of families, of whips and thumbscrews, and auction blocks; but as often as a plan was suggested by my friend, there would appear some difficulty in the way of its accomplishment. Perhaps it may not be best to mention what these plans were, as some unfortunate slaves may thereby be prevented from availing themselves of these methods of escape.

At length, after praying earnestly to Him, who seeth afar off, for assistance, in my difficulty, suddenly, as if from above, there darted into my mind these words, "Go and get a box, and put yourself in it." I pondered the words over in my mind. "Get a box?" thought I; "what can this mean?" But I was "not disobedient unto the heavenly vision," and I determined to put into practice this direction, as I considered it, from my heavenly Father.* I went to the depot, and there noticed the size of the largest boxes, which commonly were sent by the cars, and returned with their dimensions. I then repaired to a carpenter, and induced him to make me a box of such a description as I wished, informing him of the use I intended to make of it. He assured me I could not live in it; but as it was dear liberty I was in pursuit of, I thought it best to make the trial.

When the box was finished, I carried it, and placed it before my friend, who had promised to assist me, who asked me if that was to "put my clothes in?" I replied that it was not, but to "*put Henry Brown in!*" He was astonished at my temerity; but I insisted upon his placing me in it, and nailing me up, and he finally consented.

After corresponding with a friend in Philadelphia, arrangements were made for my departure, and I took my place in this narrow prison, with a mind full of uncertainty as to the result. It was a critical period of my life, I can assure you, reader; but if you have never been deprived of your liberty, as I was, you cannot realize the power of that hope of freedom, which was to me indeed, "an anchor to the soul, both sure and steadfast."

I laid me down in my darkened home of three feet by two, and like one about to be guillotined, resigned myself to my fate. My friend was to accompany me, but he failed to do so; and contented himself with sending a telegraph message to his correspondent in Philadelphia, that such a box was on its way to his care.

* Reader, smile not at the above idea, for if there is a God of love, we must believe that he suggests steps to those who apply to him in times of trouble, by which they can be delivered from their difficulty. I firmly believe this doctrine, and know it to be true from frequent experience.

I took with me a bladder filled with water to bathe my neck with, in case of too great heat; and with no access to the fresh air, excepting three small gimblet holes, I started on my perilous cruise. I was first carried to the express office, the box being placed on its end, so that I started with my head downwards, although the box was directed, "this side up with care." From the express office, I was carried to the depot, and from thence tumbled roughly into the baggage car, where I *happened* to fall "right side up," but no thanks to my transporters. But after a while the cars stopped, and I was put aboard a steamboat, *and placed on my head.* In this dreadful position, I remained the space of an hour and a half, it seemed to me, when I began to feel of my eyes and head, and found to my dismay, that my eyes were almost swollen out of their sockets, and the veins on my temple seemed ready to burst. I made no noise however, determining to obtain *"victory or death,"* but endured the terrible pain, as well as I could, sustained under the whole by the thoughts of sweet liberty. About half an hour afterwards, I attempted again to lift my hands to my face, but I found I was not able to move them. A cold sweat now covered me from head to foot. Death seemed my inevitable fate, and every moment I expected to feel the blood flowing over me, which had burst from my veins. One half hour longer and my sufferings would have ended in that fate, which I preferred to slavery; but I lifted up my heart to God in prayer, believing that he would yet deliver me, when to my joy, I overheard two men say, "We have been here *two* hours and have travelled twenty miles, now let us sit down, and rest ourselves." They suited the action to the word, and turned the box over, containing my soul and body, thus delivering me from the power of the grim messenger of death, who a few moments previously, had aimed his fatal shaft at my head, and had placed his icy hands on my throbbing heart. One of these men inquired of the other, what he supposed that box contained, to which his comrade replied, that he guessed it was the mail. "Yes," thought I, "it is a *male*, indeed, although not the *mail* of the United States."

Soon after this fortunate event, we arrived at Washington, where I was thrown from the wagon, and again as my luck would have it, fell on my head. I was then rolled down a declivity, until I reached the platform from which the cars were to start. During this short but rapid journey, my neck came very near being dislocated, as I felt it crack, as if it had snapped asunder. Pretty soon, I heard some one say, "there is no room for this box, it will have to remain behind." I then again applied to the Lord, my help in all my difficulties, and in a few minutes I heard a gentleman direct the hands to place it aboard, as "it came with the mail and must go on with it." I was then tumbled into the car, my head downwards again, as I seemed to be destined to escape on my head; a sign probably, of the opinion of American people respecting such bold adventurers as myself; that our heads should be held downwards, whenever we attempt to benefit ourselves. Not the only instance of this propensity, on the part of the American people, towards the colored race. We had not proceeded far, however, before more baggage was placed in the car, at a stopping place, and I was again turned to my proper position. No farther difficulty occurred until my arrival at Philadelphia. I reached this place at three o'clock in the morning, and remained in the depot until six o'clock, A.M., at which time, a wagon drove up, and a person inquired for a box directed to such a place, "right side up." I was soon placed on this wagon, and carried to the house of my friend's correspondent, where quite a number of persons were waiting to receive me. They appeared to be some afraid to open the box at first, but at length one of them rapped upon it, and with a trembling voice, asked, "Is all right within?" to which I replied, "All right." The joy of these friends was excessive, and like the ancient Jews, who repaired to the rebuilding of Jerusalem, each one seized hold of some tool, and commenced opening my grave. At length the cover was removed, and I arose, and shook myself from the lethargy into which I had fallen; but exhausted nature proved too much for my frame, and I swooned away.

HENRY "BOX" BROWN

2

It was the Sabbath; the holy day which God in his infinite wisdom gave for the rest of both man and beast. In the state of Maryland, the slaves generally have the Sabbath, except in those districts where the evil weed, tobacco, is cultivated; and then, when it is the season for setting the plant, they are liable to be robbed of this only rest.

It was in the month of November, somewhat past the middle of the month. It was a bright day, and all was quiet. Most of the slaves were resting about their quarters; others had leave to visit their friends on other plantations, and were absent. The evening previous I had arranged my little bundle of clothing, and had secreted it at some distance from the house. I had spent most of the forenoon in my workshop, engaged in deep and solemn thought.

It is impossible for me now to recollect all the perplexing thoughts that passed through my mind during that forenoon; it was a day of heartaching to me. But I distinctly remember the two great difficulties that stood in the way of my flight: I had a father and mother whom I dearly loved,—I had also six sisters and four brothers on the plantation. The question was, shall I hide my purpose from them? moreover, how will my flight affect them when I am gone? Will they not be suspected? Will not the whole family be sold off as a disaffected family, as is generally the case when one of its members flies? But a still more trying question was, how can I expect to succeed, I have no knowledge of distance or direction—I know that Pennsylvania is a free state, but I know not where its soil begins, or where that of Maryland ends? Indeed, at this time there was no safety in Pennsylvania, New Jersey, or New York, for a fugitive, except in lurking-places, or under the care of judicious friends, who could be entrusted not only with liberty, but also with life itself.

With such difficulties before my mind, the day had rapidly worn away; and it was just past noon. One of my perplexing questions I had settled—I had resolved to let no one into my secret; but the other difficulty was now to be met. It was to be met without the least knowledge of its magnitude, except by imagination. Yet of one thing there could be no mistake, that the consequences of a failure would be most serious. Within my recollection no one had attempted to escape from my master; but I had many cases in my mind's eye, of slaves of other planters who had failed, and who had been made examples of the most cruel treatment, by flogging and selling to the far South, where they were never to see their friends more. I was not without serious apprehension that such would be my fate. The bare possibility was impressively solemn; but the hour was now come, and the man must act and be free, or remain a slave for ever. How the impression came to be upon my mind I cannot tell; but there was a strange and horrifying belief, that if I did not meet the crisis that day, I should be self-doomed —that my ear would be nailed to the door-post for

ever. The emotions of that moment I cannot fully depict. Hope, fear, dread, terror, love, sorrow, and deep
melancholy were mingled in my mind together; my
mental state was one of most painful distraction. When
I looked at my numerous family—a beloved father
and mother, eleven brothers and sisters, etc.; but when
I looked at slavery as such; when I looked at it in its
mildest form, with all its annoyances; and above all,
when I remembered that one of the chief annoyances
of slavery, in the most mild form, is the liability of
being at any moment sold into the worst form, it
seemed that no consideration, not even that of life
itself, could tempt me to give up the thought of flight.
And then when I considered the difficulties of the way
—the reward that would be offered—the human bloodhounds that would be set upon my track—the weari-
ness—the hunger—the gloomy thought, of not only
losing all one's friends in one day, but of having to
seek and to make new friends in a strange world. But,
as I have said, the hour was come, and the man must
act, or for ever be a slave.

It was now two o'clock. I stepped into the quarter;
there was a strange and melancholy silence mingled
with the destitution that was apparent in every part
of the house. The only morsel I could see in the
shape of food, was a piece of Indian-flour bread, it
might be half-a-pound in weight. This I placed in my
pocket, and giving a last look at the aspect of the
house, and at a few small children who were playing
at the door, I sallied forth thoughtfully and melancholy, and after crossing the barn-yard, a few moments' walk brought me to a small cave, near the
mouth of which lay a pile of stones, and into which
I had deposited my clothes. From this, my course lay
through thick and heavy woods and back lands to
——town, where my brother lived. This town was
six miles distance. It was now near three o'clock, but

my object was neither to be seen on the road, or to approach the town by daylight, as I was well-known there, and as any intelligence of my having been seen there would at once put the pursuers on my track. This first six miles of my flight, I not only travelled very slowly, therefore, so as to avoid carrying any daylight to this town; but during this walk another very perplexing question was agitating my mind. Shall I call on my brother as I pass through, and shew him what I am about! My brother was older than I, we were much attached; I had been in the habit of looking to him for counsel.

I entered the town about dark, resolved, all things in view, *not* to shew myself to my brother. Having passed through the town without being recognised, I now found myself under cover of night, a solitary wanderer from home and friends; my only guide was the *north star*, by this I knew my general course north-ward, but at what point I should strike Penn., or when and where I should find a friend I knew not. Another feeling now occupied my mind,—I felt like a mariner who has gotten his ship outside of the harbour and has spread his sails to the breeze. The cargo is on board—the ship is cleared—and the voyage I must make; besides, this being my first night, almost every-thing will depend upon my clearing the coast before the day dawns. In order to do this my flight must be rapid. I therefore set forth in sorrowful earnest, only now and then I was cheered by the *wild* hope, that I should somewhere and at some time be free.

The night was fine for the season, and passed on with little interruption for want of strength, until, about three o'clock in the morning, I began to feel the chilling effects of the dew.

At this moment, gloom and melancholy again spread through my whole soul. The prospect of utter destitu-tion which threatened me was more than I could bear, and my heart began to melt. What substance is there in a piece of dry Indian-bread? what nourishment is there in it to warm the nerves of one already chilled to the heart? Will this afford a sufficient sustenance after the toil of the night? But while these thoughts were agitating my mind, the day dawned upon me, in the midst of an open extent of country, where the only shelter I could find, without risking my travel by daylight, was a corn shock, but a few hundred yards from the road, and here I must pass my first day out. The day was an unhappy one; my hiding-place was extremely precarious. I had to sit in a squatting position the whole day, without the least chance to rest. But, besides this, my scanty pittance did not afford me that nourishment which my hard night's travel needed. Night came again to my relief, and I sallied forth to pursue my journey. By this time, not a crumb of my crust remained, and I was hungry and began to feel the desperation of distress.

As I travelled I felt my strength failing and my spirits wavered; my mind was in a deep and melancholy dream. It was cloudy; I could not see my star, and had serious misgivings about my course.

In this way the night passed away, and just at the dawn of day I found a few sour apples, and took my shelter under the arch of a small bridge that crossed the road. Here I passed the second day in ambush.

This day would have been more pleasant than the previous, but the sour apples, and a draught of cold water, had produced any thing but a favourable effect; indeed, I suffered most of the day with severe symptoms of cramp. The day passed away again without any further incident, and as I set out at nightfall I felt quite satisfied that I could not pass another twenty-four hours without nourishment. I made but little progress during the night, and often sat down, and slept frequently fifteen or twenty minutes. At the dawn of the third day I continued my travel. As I had found my way to a public turnpike road during the night, I came very early in the morning to a toll-gate, where the only person I saw, was a lad about twelve years of age. I inquired of him where the road led to. He informed me it led to Baltimore. I asked him the distance, he said it was eighteen miles.

This intelligence was perfectly astounding to me. My master lived eighty miles from Baltimore. I was now sixty-two miles from home. That distance in the right direction, would have placed me several miles across Mason and Dixon's line, but I was evidently yet in the state of Maryland.

I ventured to ask the lad at the gate another question—Which is the best way to Philadelphia? Said he, you can take a road which turns off about half-a-mile below this, and goes to Getsburgh, or you can go on to Baltimore and take the packet.

I made no reply, but my thought was, that I was as near Baltimore and Baltimore-packets as would answer my purpose.

In a few moments I came to the road to which the lad had referred, and felt some relief when I had gotten out of that great public highway, "The National Turnpike," which I found it to be.

When I had walked a mile on this road, and when it had now gotten to be about nine o'clock, I met a young man with a load of hay. He drew up his horses, and addressed me in a very kind tone, when the following dialogue took place between us.

"Are you travelling any distance, my friend?"

"I am on my way to Philadelphia."

"Are you free?"

"Yes, sir."

"I suppose, then, you are provided with free papers?"

"No, sir. I have no papers."

"Well, my friend, you should not travel on this

road: you will be taken up before you have gone three miles. There are men living on this road who are constantly on the look-out for your people; and it is seldom that one escapes them who attempts to pass by day."

He then very kindly gave me advice where to turn off the road at a certain point, and how to find my way to a certain house, where I would meet with an old gentleman who would further advise me whether I had better remain till night, or go on.

I left this interesting young man; and such was my surprise and chagrin at the thought of having so widely missed my way, and my alarm at being in such a dangerous position, that in ten minutes I had so far forgotten his directions as to deem it unwise to attempt to follow them, lest I should miss my way, and get into evil hands.

I, however, left the road, and went into a small piece of wood, but not finding a sufficient hiding-place, and it being a busy part of the day, when persons were at work about the fields, I thought I should excite less suspicion by keeping in the road, so I returned to the road; but the events of the next few moments proved that I committed a serious mistake.

I went about a mile, making in all two miles from the spot where I met my young friend, and about five miles from the toll-gate to which I have referred, and I found myself at the twenty-four miles' stone from Baltimore. It was now about ten o'clock in the forenoon; my strength was greatly exhausted by reason of the want of suitable food; but the excitement that was then going on in my mind, left me little time to think of my *need* of food. Under ordinary circumstances as a traveller, I should have been glad to see the "Tavern," which was near the mile-stone; but as the case stood with me, I deemed it a dangerous place to pass, much less to stop at. I was therefore passing it as quietly and as rapidly as possible, when from the lot just opposite the house, or sign-post, I heard a coarse stern voice cry, "Halloo!"

I turned my face to the left, the direction from which the voice came, and observed that it proceeded from a man who was digging potatoes. I answered him politely; when the following occurred:—

"Who do *you* belong to?"

"I am free, sir."

"Have you got papers?"

"No, sir."

"Well, you must stop here."

By this time he had got astride the fence, making his way into the road. I said,

"My business is onward, sir, and I do not wish to stop."

"I will see then if you don't stop, you black rascal."

He was now in the middle of the road, making after me in a brisk walk.

I saw that a crisis was at hand; I had no weapons of any kind, not even a pocket-knife; but I asked myself, shall I surrender without a struggle. The instinctive answer was, "No." What will you do? continue to walk; if he runs after you, run; get him as far from the house as you can, then turn suddenly and smite him on the knee with a stone; that will render him, at least, unable to pursue you.

This was a desperate scheme, but I could think of no other, and my habits as a blacksmith had given my eye and hand such mechanical skill, that I felt quite sure that if I could only get a stone in my hand, and have time to wield it, I should not miss his knee-pan.

He began to breathe short. He was evidently vexed because I did not halt, and I felt more and more provoked at the idea of being thus pursued by a man to whom I had not done the least injury. I had just began to glance my eye about for a stone to grasp, when he made a tiger-like leap at me. This of course brought us to running. At this moment he yelled out "Jake Shouster!" and at the next moment the door of a small house standing to the left was opened, and out jumped a shoemaker girded up in his leather apron, with his knife in hand. He sprang forward and seized me by the collar, while the other seized my arms behind. I was now in the grasp of two men, either of whom were larger bodied than myself, and one of whom was armed with a dangerous weapon.

Standing in the door of the shoemaker's shop, was a third man; and in the potato lot I had passed, was still a fourth man. Thus surrounded by superior physical force, the fortune of the day it seemed to me was gone.

My heart melted away, I sunk resistlessly into the hands of my captors, who dragged me immediately into the tavern which was near. I ask my reader to go in with me, and see how the case goes.

A few moments after I was taken into the bar-room, the news having gone as by electricity, the house and yard were crowded with gossipers, who had left their business to come and see "the runaway nigger." This hastily assembled congregation consisted of men, women, and children, each one had a look to give at, and a word to say about the "nigger."

But among the whole, there stood one whose name I have never known, but who evidently wore the garb of a man whose profession bound him to speak for the dumb, but he, standing head and shoulders above all that were round about, spoke the first hard sentence against me. Said he, "That fellow is a runaway I know; put him in jail a few days, and you will soon hear where he came from." And then fixing a fiend-like gaze upon me, he continued, "if I lived on this road, *you* fellows would not find such clear running as you do, I'd trap more of you."

But now comes the pinch of the case, the case of conscience to me even at this moment. Emboldened by the cruel speech just recited, my captors enclosed me, and said, "Come now, this matter may easily be settled without you going to jail; who do you belong to, and where did you come from?"

The facts here demanded were in my breast. I knew according to the law of slavery, who I belonged to and where I came from, and I must now do one of three things—I must refuse to speak at all, or I must communicate the fact, or I must tell an untruth. How would an untutored slave, who had never heard of such a writer as Archdeacon Paley, be likely to act in such a dilemma? The first point decided was, the facts in this case are my private property. These men have no more right to them than a highway robber has to my purse. What will be the consequence if I put them in possession of the facts. In forty-eight hours, I shall have received perhaps one hundred lashes, and be on my way to the Louisiana cotton-fields. Of what service will it be to them. They will get a palty sum of two hundred dollars. Is not my liberty worth more to me than two hundred dollars are to them?

I resolved, therefore, to insist that I was free. This not being satisfactory without other evidence, they tied my hands and set out, and went to a magistrate who lived about half a mile distant. It so happened, that when we arrived at his house he was not at home. This was to them a disappointment, but to me it was a relief; but I soon learned by their conversation, that there was still another magistrate in the neighbour-hood, and that they would go to him. In about twenty minutes, and after climbing fences and jumping ditches, we, captors and captive, stood before his door, but it was after the same manner as before—he was not at home. By this time the day had worn away to one or two o'clock, and my captors evidently began to feel somewhat impatient of the loss of time. We were about a mile and a quarter from the tavern. As we set out on our return, they began to parley. Finding it was difficult for me to get over fences with my hands tied, they untied me, and said, "Now John," that being the name they had given me, "if you have run away from any one, it would be much better for you to tell us!" but I continued to affirm that I was free. I knew, however, that my situation was very critical, owing to the shortness of the distance I must be from home: my advertisement might overtake me at any moment.

On our way back to the tavern, we passed through a small skirt of wood, where I resolved to make an effort to escape again. One of my captors was walking on either side of me; I made a sudden turn, with my left arm sweeping the legs of one of my captors from under him; I left him nearly standing on his head, and took to my heels. As soon as they could recover they both took after me. We had to mount a fence. This I did most successfully, and making across an open field towards another wood; one of my captors being a long-legged man, was in advance of the other, and consequently nearing me. We had a hill to rise, and during the ascent he gained on me. Once more I thought of self-defence. I am trying to escape peaceably, but this man is determined that I shall not.

My case was now desperate; and I took this desperate thought: "I will run him a little farther from his coadjutor; I will then suddenly catch a stone, and wound him in the breast." This was my fixed purpose, and I had arrived near the point on the top of the hill, where I expected to do the act, when to my surprise and dismay, I saw the other side of the hill was not only all ploughed up, but we came suddenly upon a man ploughing, who as suddenly left his plough and cut off my flight, by seizing me by the collar, when at the same moment my pursuer seized my arms behind. Here I was again in a sad fix. By this time the other pursuer had come up; I was most savagely thrown down on the ploughed ground with my face downward, the ploughman placed his knee upon my shoulders, one of my captors put his upon my legs, while the other tied my arms behind me. I was then dragged up and marched off with kicks, punches and imprecations.

We got to the tavern at three o'clock. Here they again cooled down, and made an appeal to me to make a disclosure. I saw that my attempt to escape strengthened their belief that I was a fugitive. I said to them, "If you will not put me in jail, I will now tell you where I am from." They promised. "Well," said I, "a few weeks ago, I was sold from the eastern shore to a slave-trader, who had a large gang, and set out for Georgia, but when he got to a town in Virginia, he was taken sick, and died with the small-pox. Several of his gang also died with it, so that the people in the town became alarmed, and did not wish the gang to remain among them. No one claimed us, or wished to have anything to do with us; I left the rest, and thought I would go somewhere and get work."

When I said this, it was evidently believed by those who were present, and notwithstanding the unkind feeling that had existed, there was a murmur of approbation. At the same time I perceived that a panic began to seize some, at the idea that I was one of a small-pox gang. Several who had clustered near me, moved off to a respectful distance. One or two left the bar-room, and murmured, "better let the small-pox nigger go."

I was then asked what was the name of the slave-trader. Without premeditation, I said, "John Henderson."

"John Henderson," said one of my captors, "I knew

him; I took up a yaller boy for him about two years ago, and got fifty dollars. He passed out with a gang about that time, and the boy ran away from him at Frederickstown. What kind of a man was he?"

At a venture, I gave a description of him. "Yes," said he, "that is the man." By this time all the gossippers had cleared the coast; our friend, "Jake Shouster," had also gone back to his bench to finish his custom work, after having "lost nearly the whole day, trotting about with a nigger tied," as I heard his wife say as she called him home to his dinner. I was now left alone with the man who first called to me in the morning. In a sober manner, he made this proposal to me: "John, I have a brother living in Risterstown, four miles off, who keeps a tavern; I think you had better go and live with him, till we see what will turn up. He wants an ostler." I at once assented to this. "Well," said he, "take something to eat, and I will go with you."

Although I had so completely frustrated their designs for the moment, I knew that it would by no means answer for me to go into that town, where there were prisons, handbills, newspapers, and travellers. My intention was, to start with him, but not to enter the town alive.

I sat down to eat; it was Wednesday, four o'clock, and this was the first regular meal I had since Sunday morning. This over, we set out, and to my surprise, he proposed to walk. We had gone about a mile and a-half, and we were approaching a wood through which the road passed with a bend. I fixed upon that as the spot where I would either free myself from this man, or die in his arms. I had resolved upon a plan of operation—it was this: to stop short, face about, and commence action; and neither ask or give quarters, until I was free or dead!

We had got within six rods of the spot, when a

gentleman turned the corner, meeting us on horseback. He came up, and entered into conversation with
my captor, both of them speaking in Dutch, so that I
knew not what they said. After a few moments, this
gentleman addressed himself to me in English, and I
then learned that he was one of the magistrates on
whom we had called in the morning; I felt that another
crisis was at hand. Using his saddle as his bench, he
put on an extremely stern and magisterial-like face,
holding up his horse not unlike a field-marshal in the
act of reviewing troops, and carried me through a
most rigid examination in reference to the statement
I had made. I repeated carefully all I had said; at the
close, he said, "Well, you had better stay among us a
few months, until we see what is to be done with you."
It was then agreed that we should go back to the
tavern, and there settle upon some further plan. When
we arrived at the tavern, the magistrate alighted from
his horse, and went into the bar-room. He took another
close glance at me, and went over some points of the
former examination. He seemed quite satisfied of the
correctness of my statement, and made the following
proposition: that I should go and live with him for a
short time, stating that he had a few acres of corn
and potatoes to get in, and that he would give me
twenty-five cents per day. I most cheerfully assented
to this proposal. It was also agreed that I should remain at the tavern with my captor that night, and that
he would accompany me in the morning. This part
of the arrangement I did not like, but of course I
could not say so. Things being thus arranged, the
magistrate mounted his horse, and went on his way
home.

It had been cloudy and rainy during the afternoon,
but the western sky having partially cleared at this
moment, I perceived that it was near the setting of
the sun.

My captor had left his hired man most of the day to dig potatoes alone; but the waggon being now loaded, it being time to convey the potatoes into the barn, and the horses being all ready for that purpose, he was obliged to go into the potato field and give assistance.

I should say here, that his wife had been driven away by the small-pox panic about three o'clock, and had not yet returned; this left no one in the house, but a boy, about nine years of age.

As he went out, he spoke to the boy in Dutch, which I supposed, from the little fellow's conduct, to be instructions to watch me closely, which he certainly did.

The potato lot was across the public road, directly in front of the house; at the back of the house, and about 300 yards distant, there was a thick wood. The circumstances of the case would not allow me to think for one moment of remaining there for the night—the time had come for another effort—but there were two serious difficulties. One was, that I must either deceive or dispatch this boy who is watching me with intense vigilance. I am glad to say, that the latter did not for a moment seriously enter my mind. To deceive him effectually, I left my coat and went to the back door, from which my course would be direct to the wood. When I got to the door, I found that the barn, to which the waggon must soon come, lay just to the right, and overlooking the path I must take to the wood. In front of me lay a garden surrounded by a picket fence, to the left of me was a small gate, and that by passing through that gate would throw me into an open field, and give me clear running to the wood; but on looking through the gate, I saw that my captor, being with the team, would see me if I attempted to start before he moved from the position he then occupied. To add to my difficulty the horses had baulked;

while waiting for the decisive moment, the boy came to the door and asked me why I did not come in. I told him I felt unwell, and wished him to be so kind as to hand me a glass of water; expecting while he was gone to get it, the team would clear, so that I could start. While he was gone, another attempt was made to start the team but failed; he came with the water and I quickly used it up by gargling my throat and by drinking a part. I asked him to serve me by giving me another glass: he gave me a look of close scrutiny, but went in for the water. I heard him fill the glass, and start to return with it; when the hind end of the waggon cleared the corner of the house, which stood in a range with the fence along which I was to pass in getting to the wood. As I passed out the gate, I "squared my main-yard," and laid my course up the line of fence, I cast a last glance over my right shoulder, and saw the boy just perch his head above the garden picket to look after me; I heard at the same time great confusion with the team, the rain having made the ground slippery, and the horses having to cross the road with a slant and rise to get into the barn, it required great effort after they started to prevent their baulking. I felt some assurance that although the boy might give the alarm, my captor could not leave the team until it was in the barn. I heard the horses' feet on the barn-floor, just as I leaped the fence, and darted into the wood.

The sun was now quite down behind the western horizon, and just at this time a heavy dark curtain of clouds was let down, which seemed to usher in haste the night shade. I have never before or since seen anything which seemed to me to compare in sublimity with the spreading of the night shades at the close of that day. My reflections upon the events of that day, and upon the close of it, since I became acquainted with the Bible, have frequently brought to my mind that beautiful passage in the Book of Job, "He holdeth back the face of His throne, and spreadeth a cloud before it."

Before I proceed to the critical events and final deliverance of the next chapter, I cannot forbear to pause a moment here for reflection. The reader may well imagine how the events of the past day affected my mind. You have seen what was done to me; you have heard what was said to me—you have also seen what I have done, and heard what I have said. If you ask me whether I had expected before I left home, to gain my liberty by shedding men's blood, or breaking their limbs? I answer, No! and as evidence of this, I had provided no weapon whatever; not so much as a penknife—it never once entered my mind. I cannot say that I expected to have the ill fortune of meeting with any human being who would attempt to impede my flight.

If you ask me if I expected when I left home to gain my liberty by fabrications and untruths? I answer, No! my parents, slaves as they were, had always taught me, when they could, that "truth may be blamed but cannot be ashamed;" so far as their example was concerned, I had no habits of untruth. I was arrested, and the demand made upon me, "Who do you belong to?" Knowing the fatal use these men would make of *my* truth, I at once concluded that they had no more right to it than a highwayman has to a traveller's purse.

If you ask me whether I now really believe that I gained my liberty by those lies? I answer, No! I now believe that I should be free, had I told the truth; but, at that moment, I could not see any other way to baffle my enemies, and escape their clutches.

The history of that day has never ceased to inspire me with a deeper hatred of slavery; I never recur to it but with the most intense horror at a system which can put a man not only in peril of liberty, limb, and life itself, but which may even send him in haste to the bar of God with a lie upon his lips.

Whatever my readers may think, therefore, of the history of events of the day, do not admire in it the fabrications; but *see* in it the impediments that often fall into the pathway of the flying bondman. *See* how human bloodhounds gratuitously chase, catch, and tempt him to shed blood and lie; how when he would do good, evil is thrust upon him.

Almost immediately on entering the wood, I not only found myself embosomed in the darkness of the night, but I also found myself entangled in a thick forest of undergrowth, which had been quite thoroughly wetted by the afternoon rain.

I penetrated through the wood, thick and thin, and more or less wet, to the distance I should think of three miles. By this time my clothes were all thoroughly soaked through, and I felt once more a gloom and wretchedness; the recollection of which makes me shudder at this distant day. My young friends in this highly favoured Christian country, surrounded with all the comforts of home and parental care, visited by pastors and Sabbath-school teachers, think of the dreary condition of the blacksmith boy in the dark wood that night; and then consider that thousands of his brethren have had to undergo much greater hardships in their flight from slavery.

I was now out of the hands of those who had so cruelly teased me during the day; but a number of fearful thoughts rushed into my mind to alarm me. It was dark and cloudy, so that I could not see the *north star*. How do I know what ravenous beasts are in this wood? How do I know what precipices may be within its bounds? I cannot rest in this wood to-morrow, for it will be searched by those men from whom I have escaped; but how shall I regain the road?

How shall I know when I am on the right road again?

These are some of the thoughts that filled my mind with gloom and alarm.

At a venture I struck an angle northward in search of the road. After several hours of zigzag and laborious travel, dragging through briars, thorns and running vines, I emerged from the wood and found myself wading marshy ground and over ditches.

I can form no correct idea of the distance I travelled, but I came to a road, I should think about three o'clock in the morning. It so happened that I came out near where there was a fork in the road of three prongs.

Now arose a serious query—Which is the right prong for me? I was reminded by the circumstance of a superstitious proverb among the slaves, that "the left-hand turning was unlucky," but as I had never been in the habit of placing faith in this or any similar superstition, I am not aware that it had the least weight upon my mind, as I had the same difficulty with reference to the right-hand turning. After a few moments parley with myself, I took the central prong of the road and pushed on with all my speed.

It had not cleared off, but a fresh wind had sprung up; it was chilly and searching. This with my wet clothing made me very uncomfortable; my nerves began to quiver before the searching wind. The barking of mastiffs, the crowing of fowls, and the distant rattling of market waggons, warned me that the day was approaching.

My British reader must remember that in the region where I was, we know nothing of the long hours of twilight you enjoy here. With us the day is measured more by the immediate presence of the sun, and the night by the prevalence of actual darkness.

The day dawned upon me when I was near a small house and barn, situate close to the road-side. The barn was too near the road, and too small to afford secure shelter for the day; but as I cast my eye around by the dim light, I could see no wood, and no larger barn. It seemed to be an open country to a wide extent. The sun was travelling so rapidly from his eastern chamber, that ten or fifteen minutes would spread broad daylight over my track. Whether *my* deed was evil, *you* may judge, but I freely confess that I did *then* prefer darkness rather than light; I therefore took to the mow of the little barn at a great risk, as the events of the day will shew. It so happened that the barn was filled with corn fodder, newly cured and lately got in. You are aware that however quietly one may crawl into such a bed, he is compelled to make much more noise than if it were a feather-bed; and also considerably more than if it were hay or straw. Besides inflicting upon my own excited imagination the belief that I made noise enough to be heard by the inmates of the house who were likely to be rising at the time, I had the misfortune to attract the notice of a little house-dog, such as we call in that part of the world a "fice," on account of its being not only the smallest species of the canine race, but also, because it is the most saucy, noisy, and teasing of all dogs. This little creature commenced a fierce barking. I had at once great fears that the mischievous little thing would betray me; I fully apprehended that as soon as the man of the house arose, he would come and make search in the barn. It now being entirely daylight, it was too late to retreat from this shelter, even if I could have found another; I, therefore, bedded myself down into the fodder as best I could, and entered upon the annoyances of the day, with the frail hope to sustain my mind.

It was Thursday morning; the clouds that had veiled the sky during the latter part of the previous day and the previous night were gone. It was not until about an hour after the sun rose that I heard any out-door movements about the house. As soon as I heard those movements, I was satisfied there was but one man about the house, and that he was preparing to go some distance to work for the day. This was fortunate for me; the busy movements about the yard, and especially the active preparations in the house for breakfast, silenced my unwelcome little annoyer, the fice, until after the man had gone, when he commenced afresh, and continued with occasional intermissions through the day. He made regular sallies from the house to the barn, and after smelling about, would fly back to the house, barking furiously; thus he strove most skilfully throughout the entire day to raise an alarm. There seemed to be no one about the house but one or two small children and the mother, after the man was gone. About ten o'clock my attention was gravely directed to another trial; how could I pass the day without food. The reader will remember it is Thursday, and the only regular meal I have taken since Sunday, was yesterday in the midst of great agitation, about four o'clock; that since that I have performed my arduous night's travel. At one moment, I had nearly concluded to go and present myself at the door, and ask the woman of the house to have compassion and give me food; but then I feared the consequences might be fatal, and I resolved to suffer the day out. The wind sprang up fresh and cool; the barn being small and the crevices large, my wet clothes were dried by it, and chilled me through and through.

I cannot now, with pen or tongue, give a correct idea of the feeling of wretchedness I experienced; every nerve in my system quivered, so that not a particle of my flesh was at rest. In this way I passed the day till about the middle of the afternoon, when there seemed to be an unusual stir about the public road, which passed close by the barn. Men seemed to be passing in parties on horseback, and talking anxiously. From a word which I now and then overheard, I had not a shadow of doubt that they were in search of me. One I heard say, "I ought to catch such a fellow, the only liberty he should have for one fortnight, would be ten feet of rope." Another I heard say, "I reckon he is in that wood now." Another said, "Who would have thought that rascal was so 'cute?" All this while the little fice was mingling his voice with those of the horsemen, and the noise of the horses' feet. I listened and trembled.

Just before the setting of the sun, the labouring man of the house returned, and commenced his evening duties about the house and barn; chopping wood, getting up his cow, feeding his pigs, etc., attended by the little brute, who continued barking at short intervals. He came several times into the barn below. While matters were passing thus, I heard the approach of horses again, and as they came up nearer, I was led to believe that all I had heard pass were returning in one party. They passed the barn and halted at the house, when I recognized the voice of my old captor; addressing the labourer, he asked, "Have you seen a runaway nigger pass here today?"

LABOURER.—"No; I have not been at home since early this morning. Where did he come from?"

CAPTOR.—"I caught him down below here yesterday morning. I had him all day, and just at night he fooled me and got away. A party of us have been after him all day; we have been up to the line, but can't hear or see any thing of him. I heard this morning where he came from. He is a blacksmith, and a stiff reward is out for him—two hundred dollars."

LABOURER.—"He is worth looking for."

CAPTOR.—"I reckon so. If I get my clutches on him again, I'll mosey* him down to —— before I eat or sleep."

Reader, you may if you can, imagine what the state

* An expression which signifies to drive in a hurry.

of my mind was at this moment. I shall make no attempt to describe it to you; to my great relief, however,
the party rode off, and the labourer after finishing his
work went into the house. Hope seemed now to dawn
for me once more; darkness was rapidly approaching,
but the moments of twilight seemed much longer than
they did the evening before. At length the sable covering had spread itself over the earth. About eight
o'clock I ventured to descend from the mow of the
barn into the road. The little dog the while began a
furious fit of barking, so much so, that I was sure
that with what his master had learned about me, he
could not fail to believe I was about his premises. I
quickly crossed the road, and got into an open field
opposite. After stepping lightly about two hundred
yards, I halted, and on listening, I heard the door
open. Feeling about on the ground, I picked up two
stones, and one in each hand I made off as fast as I
could, but I heard nothing more that indicated pursuit, and after going some distance I discharged my
encumbrance, as from the reduced state of my bodily
strength, I could not afford to carry ballast.

This incident had the effect to start me under great
disadvantage to make a good night's journey, as it
threw me at once off the road, and compelled me to
encounter at once the tedious and laborious task of
beating my way across marshy fields, and to drag
through woods and thickets where there were no
paths.

After several hours I found my way back to the
road, but the hope of making any thing like clever
speed was out of the question. All I could do was to
keep my legs in motion, and this I continued to do with
the utmost difficulty. The latter part of the night I suffered extremely from cold. There came a heavy frost;
I expected at every moment to fall on the road and
perish. I came to a corn-field covered with heavy

shocks of Indian corn that had been cut; I went into this and got an ear, and then crept into one of the shocks; ate as much of it as I could, and thought I would rest a little and start again, but weary nature could not sustain the operation of grinding hard corn for its own nourishment, and I sunk to sleep.

When I awoke, the sun was shining around; I started with alarm, but it was too late to think of seeking any other shelter; I therefore nestled myself down, and concealed myself as best I could from the light of day. After recovering a little from my fright, I commenced again eating my whole corn. Grain by grain I worked away at it; when my jaws grew tired, as they often did, I would rest, and then begin afresh. Thus, although I began an early breakfast, I was nearly the whole of the forenoon before I had done.

Nothing of importance occurred during the day, until about the middle of the afternoon, when I was thrown into a panic by the appearance of a party of gunners, who passed near me with their dogs. After shooting one or two birds, however, and passing within a few rods of my frail covering, they went on, and left me once more in hope. Friday night came without any other incident worth naming. As I sallied out, I felt evident benefit from the ear of corn I had nibbled away. My strength was considerably renewed; though I was far from being nourished, I felt that my life was at least safe from death by hunger. Thus encouraged, I set out with better speed than I had made since Sunday and Monday night. I had a presentiment, too, that I must be near free soil. I had not yet the least idea where I should find a home or a friend, still my spirits were so highly elated, that I took the whole of the road to myself; I ran, hopped, skipped, jumped, clapped my hands, and talked to myself. But to the old slaveholder I had left, I said, "Ah! ah! old fellow, I told you I'd fix you."

After an hour or two of such freaks of joy, a gloom would come over me in connexion with these questions, "But where are you going? What are you going to do? What will you do with freedom without father, mother, sisters, and brothers? What will you say when you are asked where you were born? You know nothing of the world; how will you explain the fact of your ignorance?

These questions made me feel deeply the magnitude of the difficulties yet before me.

Saturday morning dawned upon me; and although my strength seemed yet considerably fresh, I began to feel a hunger somewhat more destructive and pinching, if possible, than I had before. I resolved, at all risk, to continue my travel by day-light, and to ask information of the first person I met.

The events of the next chapter will shew what fortune followed this resolve.

The resolution of which I informed the reader at the close of the last chapter, being put into practice, I continued my flight on the public road; and a little after the sun rose, I came in sight of a toll-gate again. For a moment all the events which followed my passing a toll-gate on Wednesday morning, came fresh to my recollection, and produced some hesitation; but at all events, said I, I will try again.

On arriving at the gate, I found it attended by an elderly woman, whom I afterwards learned was a widow, and an excellent Christian woman. I asked her if I was in Pennsylvania. On being informed that I was, I asked her if she knew where I could get employ? She said she did not; but advised me to go to W. W., a Quaker, who lived about three miles from her, whom I would find to take an interest in me. She gave me directions which way to take; I thanked her, and bade her good morning, and was very careful to follow her directions.

In about half an hour I stood trembling at the door of W. W. After knocking, the door opened upon a comfortably spread table; the sight of which seemed at once to increase my hunger sevenfold. Not daring to enter, I said I had been sent to him in search of employ. "Well," said he, "Come in and take thy breakfast, and get warm, and we will talk about it; thee must be cold without any coat." *"Come in and take thy breakfast, and get warm!"* These words spoken by a stranger, but with such an air of simple sincerity and fatherly kindness, made an overwhelming impression upon my mind. They made me feel, spite of all my fear and timidity, that I had, in the providence of God, found a friend and a home. He at once gained my confidence; and I felt that I might confide to him a fact which I had, as yet, confided to no one.

From that day to this, whenever I discover the least disposition in my heart to disregard the wretched condition of any poor or distressed persons with whom I meet, I call to mind these words—*"Come in and take thy breakfast, and get warm."* They invariably remind me of what I was at that time; my condition was as wretched as that of any human being can possibly be, with the exception of the loss of health or reason. I had but four pieces of clothing about my person, having left all the rest in the hands of my captors. I was a starving fugitive, without home or friends—a reward offered for my person in the public papers—pursued by cruel man-hunters, and no claim upon him to whose door I went. Had he turned me away, I must have perished. Nay, he took me in, and gave me of his food, and shared with me his own garments. Such treatment I had never before received at the hands of any white man.

JAMES W. C. PENNINGTON